Changing the Guard

Recent Titles in STUDIES IN CRIME AND PUBLIC POLICY
Michael Tonry and Norval Morris, General Editors

David H. Bayley

Changing the Guard

Developing Democratic Police Abroad

OXFORD
UNIVERSITY PRESS

2006

OXFORD
UNIVERSITY PRESS

Oxford University Press, Inc., publishes works that further
Oxford University's objective of excellence
in research, scholarship, and education.

Oxford   New York
Auckland   Cape Town   Dar es Salaam   Hong Kong   Karachi
Kuala Lumpur   Madrid   Melbourne   Mexico City   Nairobi
New Delhi   Shanghai   Taipei   Toronto

With offices in
Argentina   Austria   Brazil   Chile   Czech Republic   France   Greece
Guatemala   Hungary   Italy   Japan   Poland   Portugal   Singapore
South Korea   Switzerland   Thailand   Turkey   Ukraine   Vietnam

Copyright © 2006 by Oxford University Press, Inc.

Published by Oxford University Press, Inc.
198 Madison Avenue, New York, New York 10016

www.oup.com

Oxford is a registered trademark of Oxford University Press

Library of Congress Cataloging-in-Publication Data
Bayley, David H.
Changing the guard : developing democratic police abroad / by David H. Bayley.
p. cm. — (Studies in crime and public policy)
ISBN-13 978-0-19-518975-9

1. Police—International cooperation. 2. Police—Developing countries.
3. Technical assistance, American. 4. Technical assistance—Developing countries.
5. Democratization. 6. Law reform. I. Title. II. Series.
HV7921.B39 2005
363.2'09172'4—dc22   2005004301

Printed in the United States of America
on acid-free paper

Preface

This book examines the policies and practices involved in assisting countries to develop democratic policing. It is a "how-to" book, pinpointing the lessons that have been learned about both the substance and practice of providing assistance to the police and, more largely, the justice sector.

This book brings together the two major interests of my professional life: the study of strategic change within police organizations and the comparison of international policing practices. Research for this project began in 2000 with an exhaustive survey of writing about domestic and international experience with facilitating institutional change in police agencies. Supported by the National Institute of Justice (NIJ), U.S. Department of Justice, I created a team composed of two graduate students and myself to collect writing about the process of changing police institutions. As an NIJ Fellow, I also spent two months in Washington, DC, discussing assistance issues with government policy makers and field personnel who had returned from overseas missions. This research culminated in the publication of *Democratizing the Police Abroad: What To Do and How To Do It* (2001).

During 2002–2004, I visited four countries to explore the problems of applying the lessons of assistance in real-world settings. The countries were El Salvador (2002), Bosnia-Herzegovina (2002), South Africa (2003), and Ukraine (2004). Since it was impossible to construct a scientifically valid random sample of countries to which the United States was giving police assistance, I choose countries that illustrated differences in context: El Salvador—Latin America, predominantly bilateral assistance, third-world conditions, negotiated transition to democracy; Bosnia-Herzegovina—Europe, multilateral assistance, relatively sophisticated infrastructure, peacekeeping intervention; South Africa—sub-Saharan Africa, multiple donors both bi- and multilateral, sophisticated infrastructure coupled with deep socioeconomic cleavages, negotiated transition to democracy; Ukraine—former Soviet Union, multiple bilateral programs, peaceful transition from Communism. In each country I interviewed local and foreign personnel involved in assistance projects. During this period I also visited other countries that have been major providers of police assistance (Australia, Canada, Germany, Japan, Norway, Sweden, and the United Kingdom) to assess the extent and nature of their programs and to discuss the process of assistance as they have experienced it.

Support for most of this field research was provided by the John D. and Catherine T. MacArthur Foundation. I am enormously grateful for their interest in the topic and their understanding of the peculiarities of policy research. The U.S. Institute of Peace, Washington, DC, provided financial support for the research in Ukraine, as well as brief visits to donor and training agencies in Vienna, Budapest, and Moscow.

At the end of the project, I returned to Washington to discuss my observations in the field with officials in U.S. government agencies and departments. I also used this opportunity to explore the status of police-assistance programs and related initiatives of policy and legislation. This work, too, was supported by the U.S. Institute of Peace.

I am also grateful to the Earhart Foundation, Ann Arbor, Michigan, for providing me, once again, with a grant to complete a major research project. They understand that small grants can make a big difference.

All that I have learned about changing police institutions and about developing more humane and effective policing both at home and abroad has come from seeking out and listening to people who have been involved in such work. In this project alone they number in the hundreds and come from thirteen countries. They have been extraordinarily generous in providing advice about people I should see, opening doors, sharing insights, correcting mistaken impressions, tolerating dumb questions, and providing memorable hospitality. To all of them, my heartfelt thanks.

Unless one is extraordinarily gifted in languages, research abroad requires the assistance of interpreters. I was blessed to be able to work with three gifted, intelligent, and reliable people: Patricia Elena Aguilar Javier in El Salvador, Vanessa Glodjo in Bosnia, and Victoria Zaida in Ukraine. They not only made me intelligible to others and others to me, but also were insightful guides in matters of etiquette and culture.

Johnna Christian and Eamonn Cunningham helped to assemble and summarize the extensive literature on institutional change at home and abroad that formed the basis of my NIJ monograph (2001).

I owe a special debt to Jennifer Bryant, a talented and intelligent graduate student who served as my research assistant for the final two years of the project. She assembled materials, explored databases, and painstakingly put together statistical tables.

Research that involves multiple grants, extended travel, and complicated computer gyrations depends on generous help from many people. For all of this tender loving care, I am particular grateful to Arlene DeGonzague, Andrea Downey, Karen Silinsky, and Jo Anne deSilva, all at the School of Criminal Justice, State University of New York at Albany.

Finally, none of this work could be carried out without the unfailing support of my wife. Extended research is a kind of insanity, featuring long periods of abstraction and silence. She patiently puts up with it all, for which I count myself very blessed.

Contents

Changing the Guard

1

Problem and Opportunity

What would you do if you were sent by the U.S. government to make the police more effective and democratic in a non–English-speaking, third-world country that had just emerged from a bitter and protracted civil war and was experiencing a sharp rise in criminal violence under the new regime? During the civil war an estimated 75,000 people were killed out of a population of approximately 5.9 million. The war ended with a negotiated settlement in which reform of the police figured prominently. Few details were agreed upon, however, apart from a formula for staffing the new police with officers representative of both warring factions.

The country is very poor, with a yearly per capita income of about $2,000. Twenty percent of the people are illiterate; only about 34% of children of high school age are actually enrolled in high school. Streets and roads have ragged edges where the tarmac has collapsed onto dirt shoulders. Trucks, spewing clouds of black smoke, are overloaded with people or goods. People squat in knots along the roads, waiting for buses or private vans. Trash is everywhere. In the countryside houses are mostly made of mud and adobe, tin for the more affluent. Women carry water on their heads in large, brightly colored plastic containers. Beggars and vendors importune motorists stopped at major intersections. Women sell food and beverages out of stalls thatched with straw set on spindly poles. At night, the stalls and huts are lit by kerosene lamps and fluorescent strips, creating flickering worlds in an ocean of darkness.

The police are corrupt and often thoughtlessly brutal. They are paid miserably and work long hours in ill-equipped, dilapidated buildings. Generally unresponsive to the needs of the people, they are both feared and ridiculed. When traffic jams occur, people joke that a police officer must be directing traffic ahead. Crime—in particular, kidnappings for ransom—has risen sharply since the election of a new government. Foreigners are advised not to walk outside at night, private guards are common at businesses, and houses are surrounded by solid masonry walls topped with razor wire and broken glass.

In order to create a more effective, honest, and humane police, you have been given a budget of under a million dollars a year by the American government to pay the salaries of yourself and a staff of four, and to rent office space at the embassy. Money to support projects developed between you and the local government must be raised separately from agencies of the U.S. government or international institutions. Because the reputation of the American government is very high, however, and the needs of the country are so pressing, you have access to the highest levels of the police and government.

In these circumstances, what would you do to create capable, humane policing that is accountable to local government?

Another case: What would you do if you were sent by the United Nations (UN) as a senior executive in its civilian police force (CIVPOL) to create a new, effective, legitimate, and democratic police force in a non–English-speaking, moderately developed country that had been devastated by ethnic warfare? It has been estimated that out of a prewar population of approximately 4.5 million, 279,000 people died or are still missing and a further 2.5 million were displaced, 1.3 million of them abroad. The countryside is heavily mined, so that people don't stray from well-marked roads and paths. Everyone has a story to tell about family members who have been killed in the war. Issues of ethnicity color every decision, as everyone keeps score of group wins and losses. In the rare meetings of people from the bitterly divided ethnic groups, foreigners are taken aside to be told "the true story" by spokesmen from each group in turn.

The country is small, depressed, and wartorn, but developmentally first world, with high literacy and a substantial middle and professional class. Clothes are neat but threadbare. The organization of the new government has been jury-rigged to reflect both the aspirations of the international community for national cohesion and the substantial ethnic segregation that the war has produced. Sensible plans for reconstruction founder repeatedly on the politics of regional ethnic fiefdoms.

Scenically, the countryside is spectacular, presenting views of mountains and lakes interspersed with orderly farms and villages. Public facilities are modern, though hard-used. Streets are clean, and the orderly traffic is composed of cars, buses, and trams, not the donkeys, carts, scooters, and private transport-vans one finds in poorer countries. Food is recognizably Western, plentiful if one has money, and ice cream shops abound. Cigarette smoking is ubiquitous and the smokers are unapologetic.

You arrive in a UN-leased Russian turbojet that disconcertingly fills with smoke on takeoff. Not to worry, the loadmaster says, this is routine. You do not speak the local language and interpreters are in short supply. You are part of an enormous contingent of international agencies—the United Nations (UN), the United Nations High Commissioner for Refugees (UNHCR), the Organization for Security & Cooperation in Europe (OSCE), the World Bank, the World Health Organization (WHO), and the European Union (EU). The international agencies compete with personnel from national governments as well as private foundations for office space, housing, interpreters, supplies, transportation, and access to bewildered local officials. UN vehicles, white with black letters, fill the street like a blizzard, interspersed with North American Treaty Organization (NATO) military vehicles painted with jungle camouflage. Military personnel from many nations, distinguished by shoulder patches, mix with UN police in blue berets and with well-dressed civilians, obviously foreign, in shirts, coats, and ties. Under your nominal command, you have approximately 1,800 UN civilian police (UNCIVPOL) with which to monitor local police activities, report abuses of human rights, tutor local commanders in democratic policing, and advise, and sometimes direct, policy makers in developing effective and democratic police practices.

Since the UN has no manual on democratic policing when you arrive, where do you begin? How do you harmonize policing doctrines among UN personnel from 34 countries, many of these countries minimally democratic themselves, and then implant that with local police who are notoriously inept and corrupt. Finally, how do you convince suspicious local officials, traumatized by war but proud of their standing as a developed nation, that they have anything important to learn from disorganized, questionably competent foreigners who may not stay very long?

These two situations, and others like them, are real. Experienced, intelligent, dedicated people are being sent daily by the American government, the United Nations, and other international institutions into just these sorts of circumstances. What can such people do to facilitate the creation of democratic policing? Is it realistic to expect that they can succeed?

This book will try to answer these questions. Specifically, it will examine the prospects for reforming the police abroad as a means of encouraging the development of democratic governments. It will focus particularly on the activities of the U.S. government while drawing on the experience of several other major donors as well as multilateral organizations.

Current Activity

It is important, even urgent, to analyze this topic now because we are in a period of unprecedented effort to expand democratic institutions around the world, with the explicit recognition that reform of the police, and of the larger criminal justice system, is a critical component. During the 1990s, the international community either bilaterally or multilaterally attempted to reform, or in some cases recreate, police forces in Bosnia-Herzegovina, Cambodia, East Timor, El Salvador, Guatemala, Haiti, Kosovo, Mozambique, Namibia, Nicaragua, Panama, Sierra Leone, Somalia, and South Africa. These efforts were often part of peacekeeping operations by the United Nations, which also increased substantially during the 1990s. Fifty-four peacekeeping missions have been undertaken by the UN since 1948, 38 of them (70%) since 1990 (United Nations 2002a). UN peacekeeping often involves the insertion of UN civilian police, deployed in their now familiar light-blue berets. In early 2004, the United Nations deployed over 4000 civilian police in eight missions (Serafino 2004). The number of UNCIVPOL personnel increased from 35 in 1980 to 3,600 in 1997 and 6,181 in 2002 (United Nations 2002b). The number peaked in 2001 at 7,667.

The UN civilian police have not only grown in numerical strength in recent years but their role in peacekeeping missions has also expanded (Hansen 2002b; Serafino 2004). The traditional role of UNCIVPOL until about the middle of the 1990s was to monitor the behavior of indigenous police on the expectation that systematic observations would discourage repressive behavior. Monitoring gradually took on a more active character as UNCIVPOL began to report the misbehavior of individual local police officers, "naming and shaming," thereby initiating administrative or legal sanctions. In 1995 UNCIVPOL added advising and training of local police to their roster of activities. The doctrine was referred to as SMART: Support for human rights, Monitoring And Reporting, and advising and Training. Finally, UNCIVPOL assumed authority to enforce law on their own, and were armed for the purpose. This occurred first in Haiti (1994), then in Kosovo (1999), and later in East Timor (2001) (Perito 2003).

During the 1990s, the template for police reform and reconstruction in foreign countries was developed and codified for the first time. It is now universally referred to as "democratic policing." Little more than a mantra in the beginning, democratic policing was first defined by UNCIVPOL in Bosnia-Herzegovina in 1996 (Blair and Dziedzic 1997; Robert M. Perito 2003; United Nations Mission in Bosnia and Herzegovina 1996). UNCIVPOL's seven principles of democratic policing became the basis for *The Commissioner's Guidance for Democratic Policing in the Federation of Bosnia-Herzegovina* (United Nations Mission in Bosnia and Herzegovina 1996), which was the first detailed plan for implementing democratic police reform.[1] Democratic policing has since become synonymous with adherence to international principles of human rights as outlined in *International Human Rights Standards for Law Enforcement: A Pocket Book on Human Rights for the Police* (United Nations High Commissioner for Human Rights 1996) and *European Code of Police Ethics* (Council of Europe 2001).

The United Nations is not the only multilateral organization that developed the capacity to assist in reforming police forces abroad during the 1990s. Others include the Organization for Security and Cooperation in Europe, which created and ran the new police academy in Kosovo, and the European Union, which took over CIVPOL responsibilities from the United Nations in Bosnia-Herzegovina in 2003. The EU has created a rapid-reaction force of 1,400 police officers, which can be deployed within thirty days, supported by a reserve of 5,000 officers (U.S. Institute of Peace 2004).

American assistance in developing and reforming foreign police forces has also developed substantially in recent years, beginning with the creation of the International Criminal Investigative Training Assistance Program (ICITAP) in 1986. By 2004 the U.S. government was spending about $634 million per year on police assistance,[2] training police from over 120 countries in programs that enrolled as many as 12,000 officers each year. The United States has also contributed a large number of police to UNCIVPOL, which reached a high of 850 American officers in 2000 when large operations were being conducted in Bosnia-Herzegovina, Kosovo, and East Timor (U.S. Institute of Peace 2004). By 2004, more than 500 American police were serving with UN missions. The United States has also undertaken its own unilateral efforts to reconstruct local police in Panama (1989), Afghanistan (2001), and, most recently, Iraq (2003).

---

1. These principles were: (1) police must be oriented and operated in accordance with the principles of democracy; (2) police, as recipients of public trust, are professionals whose conduct must be governed by a professional code of conduct; (3) police must have as their highest priority the protection of life; (4) police must serve the community and are accountable to the community they serve; (5) protection of life and property is the primary function of police operations; (6) police must conduct their activities with respect for human dignity and the basic human rights of all persons; and (7) police must discharge their duties in a non-discriminatory manner.

2. This is an estimate, the basis for which is discussed in detail in chapter 3.

Altogether, 1,074 American police were serving in peacekeeping and stability operations abroad in September 2004 under either bilateral or multilateral auspices (U.S. Department of State, Bureau of International Narcotics and Law Enforcement Affairs 2004).

Bilateral assistance to police has become a worldwide undertaking. Other major participants include Britain, Canada, Denmark, France, Germany, Japan, Norway, and Sweden.

Finally, police reform has belatedly been recognized as an essential part of economic development. The World Bank, the International Monetary Fund, the European Union, and the Organisation for Economic Co-operation and Development (OECD) have all published reports about the importance of internal security for economic growth (Ball 2001; Wulf 2000). National development agencies, such as the U.S. Agency for International Development (USAID) and Great Britain's Department for International Development (DFID), have also taken explicit note of the connection between effective law enforcement and poverty reduction (Ignatieff 2002).

In sum, during the 1990s, international assistance to police development and reform according to democratic principles became a major component of foreign policy and a substantial industry for the international community collectively as well as for many, primarily first world, countries.

Political Context

What accounts for this recent flurry of concern about the character as well as the capacity of policing in foreign countries? There are several reasons. First, the ending of the Cold War (1989) transformed the search for security by the major powers. Rather than enlisting allies into coalitions of Communist and anti-Communist countries, foreign policy was refocused on reducing international disorder—ethnic cleansing, illegal migration, organized crime—that arose from civil wars, humanitarian emergencies, and failed governments (Call 1999a; Carnegie Commission on Preventing Deadly Violence 1995). A dramatic indication of this reorientation in world politics was the unprecedented willingness of the Security Council to authorize collective peacekeeping interventions (Myall 1996; Taub

2004). This increase cannot be explained by increases in conflict. Since World War II, conflicts between countries peaked at about 40 in 1986, while conflicts within countries declined from 140 to 100 between 1994 and 2000 (Gurr, Marshall, and Khosla 2001). Furthermore, while fourteen wars were contained during the Cold War, usually because rebels were defeated by indigenous governments, an equal number were contained in the 1990s by internationally brokered negotiations and peacekeeping.

Second, with the fall of the Berlin Wall in 1989 and the collapse of the Soviet Union in 1991, Communism became discredited and democracy was accepted as the form of government most conducive to civic stability, economic prosperity, and international peace. Creating democratic governments became the overarching goal of American foreign assistance as well as multilateral interventions.

Third, with the ascension of democracy as the dominant goal of political development, views about the role of police in government changed. Rather than being seen as a necessary evil, a standing threat to freedom, police became co-producers of a desirable political order. As a result, assistance to security institutions abroad, apart from the military, was no longer viewed as dangerous, unsavory, diversionary, and politically retrograde, but as a key component of social stability and economic development.

Fourth, concern about "failed" states, which could harbor international terrorists and criminal organizations, supported an interventionist foreign policy whose goal was the creation of effective, human-rights supporting, democratic governments. The United States in particular expanded this concern to "rogue" states, countries that actively promote international instability or developed weapons of mass destruction. This was the rationale for invading Iraq in 2003. The world was learning that effective, stable, and hopefully democratic government could not be achieved without reconstructing the police.

For a variety of reasons, then, criminal justice reform, in particular that of the police, became an important element in the foreign policy of the developed world during the last decade of the 20th century. I do not mean to suggest that concern with the expansion of democracy in the world has not occurred at other times. That has been a self-conscious goal of American governments in both the 19th and 20th centuries. Nor would it be correct to imply that countries, including the United States, haven't created and reformed foreign police before the 1990s. European countries did so in their overseas colonies throughout the 19th century; the United States did in the Philippines, Cuba, and Central America in the early 20th century; and the United States and its European allies introduced far-reaching reforms of the police during their occupations of Germany and Japan after World War II.

My point, more precisely, is that in the 1990s the international community rediscovered a lesson that had become marginalized during the Cold War, namely, the importance for peace and prosperity of creating effective law-enforcement institutions that operate under the rule of law and with respect for human rights. The 1990s were unique in the scope and explicitness of attention given by the international community to police reform of a democratic character.

What Is Known

Although the importance of police reform has been widely accepted in recent years, very little attention has been given to the process for achieving it. For example, in writing about peacekeeping, three phases in the creation of effective security have been distinguished: (1) military suppression of organized conflict; (2) establishment of an interim civilian police force by the intervening countries to enforce law, prevent crime, and maintain order; and (3) creation of a local civilian police institution that is both competent and humane (Oakley, Dziedzic, Goldberg 1998). Most writing about peacekeeping leaves off after the second stage, when a reasonably secure environment has been created for the international community. What is singularly lacking in writing about police reconstruction and reform are prescriptions about how reliable, rights protecting, security institutions can be built for the protection of indigenous populations. In order to create new or substantially reformed local police, where does one begin? What should happen first, second, third? What shouldn't be done? This book will address this "institutional gap."

The lack of writing about this process is ironic considering the amount of self-conscious police reform that has occurred within major donor nations in the past twenty years. The United States,

Britain, Australia, Canada, and most of the countries of western Europe have all reassessed the value of their standard policing strategies and have explored a variety of new approaches, notably "community policing" (Bayley 1994; Goldstein 1990; Skogan and Frydl 2003). They have also diversified recruitment, accommodated greater external accountability, intensified internal discipline, and changed training programs. Yet this raw material of experience about institutional change has not been drawn on to formulate reform plans abroad. There has been very little cross-fertilization between home-grown insights into police reform and the imperatives of foreign assistance.

The failure to spell out the operational lessons of democratic police reform is part of a larger intellectual failing, namely, the general neglect in expert writing of the developmental aspects of security institutions, with the exception of the military (Call 1999a; Bayley 1985; Wulf 2000). And the same is true for writing about the process for developing political democracy through foreign assistance. As Thomas Carothers has said, there is "little help from any body of learning other than occasional reports containing lists of anodyne lessons learned ranging from 'Be sensitive to local environment' to 'Democracy is not achieved overnight'" (1999b).

Inherent Difficulties

Desirable though democratic police reform is and as committed to it as the international community has been in the past few years, there is no denying that it is also a difficult, sensitive, and unpredictable undertaking. Reform of police institutions, as well as the construction of new ones, inevitably involves working with officials who are suspected of being incompetent, corrupt, and abusive. Moreover, the security capacity developed through foreign assistance may be put to repressive uses by whatever regime is in power, even one with aspirations to democracy. It was for these reasons that American assistance to police abroad became so badly compromised during the 1960s and early 1970s, leading the U.S. Congress to abolish USAID's Office of Public Security (1974) and to prohibit assistance to foreign police except under limited circumstances (1975) (Cottam and 1989; Huggins 1998; Rosenau 1995; Washington Office on Latin America 1995).

Development assistance to police is also likely to be controversial within donor countries. Foreign policy is multifaceted and police reform may be difficult to harmonize with other objectives. Insisting on reform abroad can jeopardize other foreign-policy goals, such as cooperation against terrorism, support for trade agreements, or the opening of markets. In addition, human rights groups, usually supportive of foreign assistance, are often reluctant to support programs that increase the capacity of the very security agencies whose misdeeds they have publicized and tried to correct.

Finally, the creation of stable democratic governments through foreign assistance, both intellectual and material, is a long shot under the best of circumstances. The conditions required for the creation of stable democracies are very demanding (Huntington 1968; Moore 1967; Lipset 1963). As a result, the record of past attempts by foreign countries to implant democratic institutions beyond their own shores is not encouraging (Carothers 1999b; Huggins 1998; Kennan 1995). According to one estimate, out of 15 countries in which the United States changed regimes through military intervention during the 20th century, only 4 produced democratic governments (Zeller 2003).

In sum, although assistance to police reform abroad is hugely consequential, it is also risky and uncertain. The foreign policy of developing and reforming police abroad sows dragon's teeth in a double sense: by improving the capability of a major institution of potential repression and by bringing into disrepute the activities of donors both at home and abroad.

The Intellectual Challenge

The international community is long past the point where it can continue to neglect the study of the process whereby police reform abroad becomes institutionalized. Assistance to the police for the purpose of facilitating transitions to democracy is happening. People are in the field now advising and, in some cases, directing the creation and reform of foreign police. So the question is no longer whether the international community will assist in democratic police reform abroad, but how well it will do the job.

There is a final reason for examining the process of achieving democratic police reform abroad at this time. The priorities of American foreign policy are undergoing a major shift in emphasis, from the expansion of democracy abroad to the safeguarding of the United States from international criminal threats, notably terrorism. Although concern about international criminal threats, especially illegal drugs, never entirely went away during the 1990s, the shock of 9/11 has produced a war mentality resembling that of the Cold War. More starkly than in the 1990s, the United States and the larger community of democratic nations are confronted with balancing the need to enlist allies against the goal of democratic reform. Both at home and abroad, security needs are taking precedence over the impulse to protect human rights. At this moment of perilous choice, understanding the possibilities as well as the limitations of foreign assistance in the service of democracy would be particularly useful. The issues of freedom and order always intersect at the police, and understanding how to be successful at democratic reform could help determine whether the interest shown in it since the early 1990s was a long-term trend or a short-lived exception in global foreign policy.

The fact that assistance may be given to the police for more than one purpose, and those purposes may conflict, is only one problem that complicates any analysis. Two others are critically important. Assistance may be given abroad either bilaterally, where it is under the complete control of the donor, or multilaterally, as part of a collaborative international effort. Furthermore, assistance may be given in two very different sets of circumstances: in countries undergoing largely peaceful political transitions and in countries where governments are being replaced following civil wars, governmental collapse, or international imposition. In the former circumstance, assistance is needed to facilitate reform; in the latter, it is needed to wholly reconstruct police institutions.

The complexity of the contemporary assistance enterprise is shown in figure 1.1. The diagram distinguishes three dimensions of assistance variation that combine in complex ways: purpose, auspices, and context. Each dimension is dichotomized. The primary purposes of American police assistance are to augment local law-

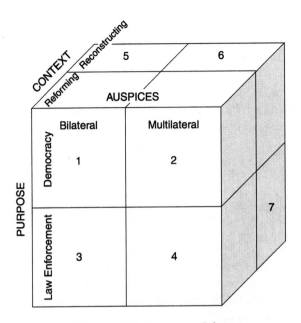

Figure 1.1 U.S. Assistance to Police

enforcement capacity or to develop democratic practices; assistance may be provided alone (bilaterally) or with others (multilaterally) and it may be provided to countries undergoing a process of largely peaceful reform and countries where government has collapsed and must be reconstructed. The category of reconstructing states encompasses both "failed states," where governments have collapsed through civil war, criminality, or incompetence, and what might be called "threat states," where governments have been overthrown by foreign invasion. Bosnia and Somalia are examples of countries where governments failed; Iraq and Afghanistan are examples of countries where functioning governments were forcibly removed because they were perceived to constitute a threat to outsiders. Obviously, contexts also vary in their historical endowments of culture, social structure, political orientations, and economic organization. While much too complicated to diagram, they too need to be considered in any assistance effort.

Most of America's police assistance effort, I shall argue later, has been in cell 3 (bilateral, law enforcement, in reforming countries), such as Ukraine, and cell 6 (multilateral, democracy, in recon-structing countries), such as Haiti, and has now expanded into cell 5 (bilateral, democracy, in reconstructing countries) and cell 8 (bilateral, law enforcement, in reconstructing countries), such as Iraq. In order to explore the process of assisting in the democratic reform of police abroad under the complex circumstances described, and to develop operational principles for doing so successfully, I shall attempt to answer the following questions:

What is democratic police reform? (chapter 2)
What is the nature and scope of American assistance to
    police abroad? (chapter 3)
What assistance strategies are most likely to achieve demo-
    cratic police reform? (chapter 4)
Can the goal of democratic reform be achieved along with
    developing the capacity of foreign police to control
    crime and disorder? (chapter 5)
How should police assistance be managed in the field?
    (chapter 6)
Have efforts at democratic police reform through foreign
    assistance been successful? (chapter 7)
What does the U.S. government need to do in order to be
    more successful at police reform abroad? (chapter 8)

The recommendations made in this book are summarized in the appendix: specifically, the nature of democratic policing, the substance of democratic police assistance, balancing reform with law enforcement, the tactics of engagement, and changes called for in the U.S. government's assistance enterprise.

2

Democracy and the Police

Reform of police forces has been central to the reconstruction of governments whether they were emerging from authoritarianism or conflict. With the collapse of Communism as an attractive philosophy of government in the late 1980s, democracy, allied with free markets, became the avowed goal of political reform worldwide. Accordingly, the dominant template for police reform is now described as democratic policing, and the encouragement of democratic police practices has become the common goal of assistance to police by the international community, whether undertaken by individual countries or under multilateral auspices.

The assumption behind the priority given to police reform in transitions to democratic government is that what the police do critically affects the character of government. It does so in two ways. First, because what the police do can so fundamentally affect the lives of citizens, especially the power to arrest and use physical force, police actions are seen as a crucial indicator of the character of gov-

17

ernment. As a simple matter of logic, it would be contradictory to say that a country was democratic if its police arbitrarily arrested people, used unreasonable force, and suppressed political dissent. Authoritarian police are the hallmarks of undemocratic governments. Second, police activity can have a profound influence not just on the judgments people make about governments but on the vitality of the processes that are essential to democratic political life, such as voting, speaking, publishing, and assembling. Police actions shape democratic political life by maintaining the boundary conditions in which it takes place.

Granting, however, that the development of democratic governments requires the creation of a democratic police, it does not follow that democratic police reform ensures the creation of democratic government (Barkan 1997; Bayley 1977, 1994, 1997; Carnegie Commission on Preventing Deadly Violence 1995; Washington Office on Latin America and American University School of International Service 1990). Democratic policing is a crucial component of democratic government, but many others things must occur to produce a viable democracy, such as regular elections, fair political competition, freedom of speech and association, and restraint in the use of governmental powers. Furthermore, any police, no matter how well trained, managed, or organizationally restructured, can be subverted by a determined government. Reform of the police is a necessary but not a sufficient condition for the creation of democratic governments. The police tail cannot wag the governmental dog.

If the development of democratic governments requires the creation of a reformed police, what are the hallmarks of such a police? What is democratic police reform? What are the changes in police institutions that foreign assistance should seek to promote in order to achieve democracy?

Essential Characteristics

In the countries that are currently most interested in assisting in its development, "democracy" refers to a government that is constitutional in the sense of being based on law, with authority exercised on behalf of representatives elected at frequent intervals by universal suffrage through processes that are free and fair (Barkan 1997; Bayley 1964;

Diamond 1995; Smith 1994; U.S. Agency for International Development 1998b; United Nations Development Programme 2002). What, then, are the institutional reforms that foreign assistance should be designed to promote in the police if democratic government in this sense is to be created? In my opinion, four reforms are crucial.

1. Police Must Be Accountable to Law Rather Than to Government

In a democracy, the actions of government are constrained by law, that is, by rules of conduct made and promulgated by elected representatives. In a democracy, police actions must be governed by the rule of law rather than by directions given arbitrarily by particular regimes and their members. Democratic police do not make law, they apply it, and any judgments must be subject to monitoring and correction by courts.

2. Police Must Protect Human Rights, Especially Those Rights That Are Required for the Sort of Political Activity That Is the Hallmark of Democracy

Democracy requires not only that the police be constrained by law but also that they make a special effort to safeguard activities that are essential to it. These are freedom of speech, association, and movement, and freedom from arbitrary arrest, detention, and exile (Annan 1998; Bayley 1964). In other words, democracy requires not only the rule of law but law with a particular content.

The rights enumerated here are what Americans call "civil rights." They regulate behavior that determines whether politics—the means by which government is regularly reconstituted—is conducted in a fair and open manner. But they do not exhaust the roster of privileges and protections that are often enshrined in law as rights and that police may need to respect. These involve cruel and unusual punishment, torture, excessive force, right to counsel, self-incrimination, speedy trial, presumption of innocence, and equality of treatment. The argument here is that although any police force must enforce the norms enacted into local law, a democratic police force must pay particular attention to the sub-set of rights that guarantee the processes of democratic government. A democratic police force must first and foremost protect those rights that determine the character of government.

The problem is that the police are not responsible for the content of law, governments are. Paradoxically, then, the obligations of the police to be accountable to the rule of law and to protect human rights may conflict, as when the law requires the police to act in a harsh and repressive way. On their own, the best that the police can do with respect to human rights is to exemplify high standards, even better than government requires, so as to show what democracy means in practice and to encourage the public to press for them.

3. *Police Must Be Accountable to People Outside Their Organization Who Are Specifically Designated and Empowered to Regulate Police Activity*

The rule of law is an empty promise if the police cannot be made accountable for it. This requires mechanisms to be established that can monitor police activity, judge its propriety, and institute remedial action as needed. This may be done by governmental bodies, such as legislatures and oversight commissions, by the legal system through courts, by the media, and by the public through non-governmental organizations.

In order for accountability to become meaningful, police activity must be open to observation and regularly reported to outsiders. This applies to information about the behavior of individual officers as well as to the operations of the institution as a whole, especially whether the police are achieving the results expected in a cost-efficient manner.

4. *Police Must Give Top Operational Priority to Servicing the Needs of Individual Citizens and Private Groups*

Police are the most visible expression of governmental authority. When they use that authority to serve primarily the interests of government they belie the democratic promise of government for the people. The most dramatic contribution police can make to democracy is to become responsive to the disaggregate needs of the populace. This is what emergency telephone systems (911 in the United States, 999 in the United Kingdom, 110 in Japan) have achieved in the developed democracies. They compel the police to attend to individual requests from citizens for assistance. In the United States, Canada, Britain, Japan, and Australia, most of the work done by the police is instigated by individual members of the public rather than by orders issued by governments. In the United States, any citizen with access to a telephone can summon a uniformed representative of the state, imbued with the authority of law and equipped with instruments of force, who will attend to his particular needs. Although police executives sometimes complain about the burden of dealing with the myriad individual calls for service, especially those that do not involve serious criminal matters, the 911 system should be viewed as a major contribution to democratic government. It represents a transformation in the orientation of police, still rare around the world, from serving regimes to serving the public.

A police force whose primary business is serving the disaggregate public supports democracy in two ways. First, it becomes accountable to the most diverse set of interests possible, namely, individual people. Second, it enhances the legitimacy of government by demonstrating that the authority of the state will be used practically and on a daily basis in the interests of the people. In most countries today, this sort of responsive, service-oriented policing would be a revolutionary departure from traditional behavior. It would, however, do more for the legitimacy of government than any other reform program, and its effects would immediately be felt.

The four criteria presented here for judging whether a police force is democratic should not be confused with particular organizational mechanisms that might be created to achieve them, such as separating the police from the military, creating internal disciplinary units, decentralizing commands, or establishing civilian review boards. A variety of organizational and managerial schemes may be adopted as means to achieve the normative end of democratizing the police. Whether they are in fact useful depends on local circumstances. Chapter 4 will explore the institutional pathways to democratic police reform that foreign assistance might support.

During the 1990s, these and other principles for creating democratic police systems were codified by several international organizations. The first was by the Commissioner for the United Nations International Police Task Force (IPTF) in Bosnia in 1996—*Commissioner's Guidance for Democratic Policing in the Federation of Bosnia-Herzegovina* (United Nations Mission in Bosnia and Herzegovina 1996). Also in 1996, the United Nations Commissioner for Human Rights issued *International Human Rights Standards for Law Enforcement: A Pocket Book on Human Rights for the Police* (United Nations

High Commissioner for Human Rights 1996). Whereas these publications dealt explicitly with democracy and human rights, others created standards for specific aspects of police conduct, such as the *Code of Conduct for Law Enforcement Officials* (1979) and *Basic Principles on the Use of Force and Firearms by Law Enforcement Officials* (1990), both from the United Nations, and the Council of Europe's *European Code of Police Ethics* (2001).

These publications represent a watershed in the development of policing. They put a normative stamp, internationally developed, on what is desirable in police practice, and in so doing, answer a question that had no definitive answer until quite recently, namely, what is democratic policing?

A Critical Caveat

There is another characteristic of a reformed police that might be regarded as essential for the creation of democratic government, namely, the development of their capacity to control crime and disorder. A government that cannot provide minimal safety to its citizens cannot be called a government, let alone a democratic one.

Instrumentally as well, personal safety is fundamental to all civil rights. The freedom to speak, publish, associate, travel, and vote may be extinguished by anarchy as well as by repressive government. Democratic government cannot be created in the face of widespread lawlessness and violent disorder.

Although I recognize that security is a requirement for democracy, both by definition and by operation, I have not made crime-control effectiveness a characteristic of a democratic police. The capacity to create order is a two-edge sword. Although it is a condition for democracy, order is not inherently democratic. It is consistent with very repressive forms of government. The rule of law, human rights, accountability, and responsiveness to citizens, however, are uniquely part of democratic practice. Being effective at maintaining essential order is necessary for police in a democratic state, but this capacity can be used both to augment and to deny political liberty. Indeed, the tension between liberty and order is a problem that all democracies face, often intensely in countries emerging from internal conflict or repression. This problem will be discussed in chapter 5.

Conclusion

Throughout this book, democratic police reform should be understood as changes in police practice along four dimensions: conformity of actions to law; adherence to international standards of human rights, especially political rights; accountability to external authority based on the capacity to collect and the willingness to publicize information about operational activities; and responsiveness to the needs of ordinary citizens. These are the institutional changes in the police that foreign assistance should give priority to in order to expand democracy around the world.

Even if these four elements are accepted as the criteria by which to judge whether police reform is democratic, there will still be sharp disagreements about whether democratic reform has taken place in particular places. People will argue about whether they have sufficient information to judge, whether unequivocal progress in one area compensates for deficiencies in another, and whether the standard for judgment should be changes measured against performance in the past or against goals for the future. Therefore, because evaluations of democratic reform are bound to be controversial despite agreement about the key criteria, I suggest a simple test of whether a police force is democratic. It is this: do parents teach their children that when the children are away from home and need help, they should seek out the police? This is a question that I have found people around the world can answer readily. It is also seen as getting at something very important about police. Finally, it is considered a fair question by police and non-police alike because it presents a goal the police can achieve. In my experience, answers to this question correspond closely to whether local police are living up to the four democratic criteria.

3

U.S. Programs and Policy

How big an enterprise is foreign assistance by the U.S. government to police abroad? What agencies do it? And what forms does it take? The fact is we don't know. At the present time, there are no authoritative estimates of the amount of police assistance, no roster of assistance programs, and no listing of the departments and agencies, or units within them, authorized to engage in such work (Neild 2001, 2004).

Why is it that there is no authoritative documentation of this strategically important and politically sensitive area of American foreign policy? Why is it that there is no comprehensive report on police assistance to foreign police? There are five reasons.

First: Responsibility for police assistance is not located in a single department or agency, nor is it a line item in the federal budget. Police assistance programs are undertaken under a series of exemptions to a blanket prohibition on providing police assistance abroad at all (Section 660[a] of the Foreign Assistance Act of 1961). It stipulates:

[N]one of the funds made available to carry out this Act, and none of the local currencies generated under this Act, shall be used to provide training or advice, or provide any financial support, for police, prisons, or other law enforcement forces for any foreign government or any program of internal intelligence or surveillance on behalf of any foreign government within the United States or abroad.

In restricting civilian foreign aid in this way, Congress was reacting against what it perceived as the misdeeds of the Office of Public Safety of the Agency for International Development from 1962 to 1974, primarily in Latin America and Vietnam (Cottam and Marenin 1989; Lewis and Marks 2000; R. M. Perito 2000; Rosenau 1995). Simplifying a complex and sobering history, American assistance had supported inhumane police strategies undertaken by repressive and undemocratic governments under the rationale of fighting Communism. Amending the Foreign Assistance Act was part of the general reconsideration of both domestic and foreign security policy that occurred in the aftermath of the Vietnam War.

Since the prohibition was enacted in 1974, it has been shredded by a series of exemptions. These come about in three ways.

1. By amendment to the Foreign Assistance Act itself. Several exemptions, for example, were built in to the amendment from the outset, most importantly for training by the Federal Bureau of Investigation (FBI) and the U.S. Department of Justice's Drug Enforcement Administration (DEA) as part of their international law enforcement activities (Section 660[b]). Starting in 1985, other exemptions were added (Section 600[b]) for: the enforcement of maritime law abroad (1985), assistance to Honduras and El Salvador for fiscal years 1986 and 1987 (now lapsed), regional security in the Eastern Caribbean (1990), monitoring and enforcement of sanctions (1996), reconstruction of civilian police in countries emerging from conflict (1996), and assistance to customs authorities.

2. By adding explicit exemptions to the Foreign Assistance Act. Referred to as "notwithstanding" clauses, explicit exemptions include Section 534 for the purpose of strengthening the administration abroad and Section 541 for mili-

tary education and training at the discretion of the President under specified circumstances.

3. By separate legislation, including annual appropriation acts, that contains "notwithstanding" exemptions. Separate legislation created, for example, the FREEDOM Support Act (FSA) in 1992,[1] the Support for East European Democracy (SEED) Act in 1989, and the Antiterrorism Assistance Program (ATA) in 2001.

So often have exemptions been granted since 1974 that many people refer to foreign police assistance as being out of control. For example, there appears to be no definitive list of the exemptions that have been made to the Section 660 prohibition. The U.S. General Accounting Office (GAO) estimated that by 1992, over 125 countries were receiving police assistance despite the ban (U.S. General Accounting Office 1992).

Second: Not only is the authorization to undertake police assistance scattered in legislation, so too are the agencies of the government that provide it. It is difficult to discover who is actually implementing police assistance programs because money provided to one agency may actually be passed on to another for implementation. As a result, an estimate of total expenditures on police assistance or, more commonly, law-enforcement assistance, cannot be produced by simply adding together items so labeled in the budgets of all government agencies. This would result in double counting. As in mystery stories, one may have to "follow the money" from appropriation bills through several agencies until arriving at the people who actually spend it. And to complicate matters, these may, in many cases, be private contactors.

In short, there is little correspondence between legislation authorizing assistance, budgetary sources of funding, authority to determine usage, and agency providers. Each must be tracked separately in order to chart the way in which police assistance is dispensed by the

---

1. The full title is Freedom for Russia and Emerging Eurasian Democracies and Open Markets Support Act. It supports exchanges of "emerging leaders," such as students and academics, and exchange programs in civics, human rights, and transparency.

U.S. government. Table 3.1 shows the separate dimensions for what I consider to be the major forms of overseas police assistance. The first column shows the legislative authorization for police assistance; the second, the appropriation act that provides the money; the third, the agency that has authority to determine how the money will be used and who will implement the program; and the fourth, some of the agencies assigned to use the money. It is important to note that although legislative authorization is dispersed, as are the agencies implementing foreign police assistance, all the money comes from the Foreign Operations Appropriation Act. Furthermore, responsibility for determining who qualifies for money under the various exemptions and which agency will implement police assistance programs is concentrated in the Department of State, specifically within the Bureau for International Law Enforcement and Narcotics Affairs (INL), supported by the Office of Legal Advisor. However, as people involved in the assistance enterprise ruefully note, everyone has their own lawyers.

Third: Police assistance is not a simple category, but covers many activities. In order to compile a roster of programs, and hence estimate total expenditures, it is necessary to make judgments about the relevance of particular programs from vague titles or descriptions. For example, police assistance may be provided by programs variously labeled rule of law, counter-narcotics, democracy development, anticrime, or national security (Interagency Working Group 2002). In fact, the phrase "police assistance" rarely appears in budgets. "Law enforcement" is a more common category, but it too leaves out a host of police-related programs. In order, therefore, to determine precisely whether money is spent for police assistance, it is necessary to examine programs in substantive detail. Such program descriptions, unfortunately, are not gathered in one place across the government or even within agencies. In order to construct a definitive inventory of all the police assistance programs of the U.S. government, and from that calculate the total amount expended, it would be necessary to go into many departments and agencies, and parts thereof, and collect by hand all the programs that involve police assistance, even if not so labeled. This would be a monumental task.

Fourth: Following the American invasions of Afghanistan (2001) and Iraq (2003), supplementary legislation has authorized the

Table 3.1
Dimensions of Police Assistance

Legislation	Budget Source	Use Authority	Providers
Foreign Assistance Act – Sect. 660 – Sect. 534	Foreign operations	DOS: INL and Legal Counsel	DOJ: FBI, DEA, and OPDAT; ICITAP; USAID private contractors
SEED	Foreign operations	DOS: Europe and Eurasia Bureau	INL; DOJ; USAID contractors
FREEDOM Support Act (authorized in the annual appropriation)	Foreign operations	DOS: Europe and Eurasia Bureau	INL; DOJ; USAID contractors
Antiterrorism Assistance Program	Foreign operations	DOS: Secretariat for Counter-terrorism	INL; DOJ; USAID contractors
International Military Education and Training ACT (IMET)	Foreign operations	DOS: Legal Counsel	DOD
Supplementary Legislation, e.g., Afghanistan, Iraq	Supplementary appropriations	DOD	DOD: public and private contractors

Department of Defense to help stabilize and reconstruct the governmental infrastructure of those countries, which necessarily includes their systems of civil and criminal justice. Much of this money is passed on to civilian agencies of the U.S. government, such as the Bureau of International Narcotics and Law Enforcement Affairs of the Department of State and the International Criminal Investigative Training Assistance Program of the Department of Justice. The amount of money involved in creating new police agencies in Afghanistan and Iraq is difficult to determine, but it can be assumed, given the colossal sums appropriated for post-conflict reconstruction, to be many orders of magnitude higher than what has been allocated through civilian agencies in both bilateral and multilateral programs.

Fifth: Assistance to police abroad may be deliberately concealed from public view, most notably with the activities of the Central Intelligence Agency (CIA). If estimates are correct that the total budget of the CIA exceeds $30 billion, a figure often mentioned, then even small allocations to police training/assistance abroad relative to their total budget could make a substantial difference to my estimate of police assistance (Central Intelligence Agency 1997).[2]

For all these reasons, it is difficult to try to determine the size and nature of governmental efforts to assist foreign police. On the other hand, because police assistance is so consequential and so politically sensitive, it is important that we have some idea about what is being done, by whom, and to what extent. In this chapter, therefore, I will (1) estimate the amount of money expended by the U.S. government on assisting police abroad, restricting my calculation, for reasons previously given, to "normal" assistance through civilian agencies; (2) describe the agencies primarily involved in providing police assistance; (3) explore the worldwide reach of police assistance; and (4) assess the character of these efforts.

Estimate of Expenditures

I estimate that in fiscal year 2004, the latest year for which data is available, the U.S. government spent approximately $635 million on the development and support of police abroad. See table 3.2. This appears to represent an enormous increase in police assistance under the Bush administration and a steady increase since the early 1990s. I say "appears to represent" because categories for reporting the largest items of direct-police support have changed since then. However, it is possible to infer the rate of growth from changes in spending by

2. In response to a lawsuit filed under the Freedom of Information Act, the director of central intelligence reported that the CIA's budget for 1997 was $26.6 billion and was projected for 1997 at $26.7 billion. Information about the CIA's budget has not been released again.

the Bureau of International Narcotics and Law Enforcement Affairs (INL) of the Department of State. This is reasonable because INL accounted for 69% of police assistance in 2004. Between FY 1993 and FY 2003, INL's budget increased sevenfold, from $147 million to $1.1 billion.[3] Compared with 1994, the increase is tenfold. It is fair to conclude that American support for foreign police today is seven to ten times larger than it was just after the end of the Cold War.

These estimates are based on information provided yearly in the Congressional Budget Justifications for Foreign Operations and for INL, both prepared by the Department of State. INL, which is a bureau with the Department of State, prepares its own more detailed budget justification because it appears as a line item in the federal budget. These two Congressional Budget Justifications cover all expenditures on justice and police abroad carried out by non-clandestine civilian agencies and by military agencies not acting under emergency legislation, such as in Afghanistan and Iraq. My estimate of expenditures, and all other generalizations in this chapter, represents, therefore, "normal" assistance to police and justice systems abroad.

In making my estimate, I have distinguished assistance given directly to police abroad (table 3.2) from more general assistance to justice institutions that could importantly affect the character and performance of the police (table 3.3). Direct assistance to foreign law-enforcement agencies substantially outweighs justice assistance generally. Clearly, policing is central to American efforts to develop, reform, and reconstruct justice systems overseas.

Referring to the tables, just over half of "normal" funding by the U.S. government for justice activities flows through the Department of State, specifically the Bureau of International Narcotics and Law Enforcement Affairs (52%—$486.7 million). INL was created in 1985 to prevent illegal drugs from entering the United States, to increase international awareness of the danger of illicit drugs, to protect the United States from international crime, and to develop the capability of foreign countries to fight international crime and illicit drugs (U.S. Department of State, Bureau of Narcotics and Law Enforcement Affairs 2002). Its budget has two main components—narcotics programs and anti-crime programs.

3. This is the earliest year for which I have reliable data.

Table 3.2
Direct Police Assistance FY2004 (in thousands)

Program	Expenditures
I. Department of State	
(A) International Narcotics and Law Enforcement Affairs	$1,197,000
(1) Andean Counterdrug Initiative (ACI)	737,587
ACI Narcotics Law Enforcement and Interdiction	*321,3231
(2) International Narcotics and Law Enforcement (INCLE)	460,274
Narcotics Law Enforcement and Interdiction[1]	*34,739
Border Control[1]	*38,700
Anti-crime Programs	*11,324
International Law Enforcement Academies (ILEA)	*14,500
(B) Antiterrorism Assistance Program	*131,428
(C) Terrorist Interdiction Program	*4,971
II. Freedom Support Act (FSA)	585,000
INL Law Enforcement[2]	*16,900
III. Support for East European Democracy (SEED)	442,375
(1) Europe Law Enforcement Program[3]	
(2) INL Law Enforcement Program[3]	*41,830
(3) INL Police Training[3]	
(4) SECI Bucharest Center[3]	
IV. Department of the Treasury	
* Treasury Technical Assistance	*18,888
V. Department of Defense, IMET Program	91,000
TOTAL of items marked with asterisks	634,603

Source: Unless otherwise indicated, all figures are from the *Congressional Budget Justification, Foreign Operations, FY2006.*

1. Department of State, International Narcotics and Law Enforcement Bureau, *Congressional Budget Justification, FY2005.*

2. Department of State, *U.S. Government Assistance to and Cooperative Activities with Eurasia, FY2003.*

3. *SEED Act Implementation Report, FY 2003.*

Table 3.3
Indirect Police Assistance FY2004 (in thousands)

Program	Expenditures
I. Department of State	
(1) ACI, Administration of Justice and Support for Democracy[1]	$33,976
(2) INCLE, Administration of Justice and Support for Democracy[1]	2,872
(3) Trafficking in Persons	12,000
II. Economic Support Fund	
Global–Human Rights and Democracy Fund	34,296
III. USAID	
(1) Democracy and Governance Office[3]	150,000
(2) Transition Initiatives	54,676
IV. Support for East European Democracy (SEED)	
(1) Criminal Justice System[2]	3,650
(2) Anti-trafficking[2]	1,430
TOTAL	292,900

Source: Unless otherwise indicated, all figures are from the *Congressional Budget Justification, Foreign Operations, FY2006*.

1. Department of State, International Narcotics and Law Enforcement, Congressional Budget Justification, FY2005.

2. *SEED Act Implementation Report, FY 2003*.

3. Private communication. Democracy and Governance has four programs—elections/ parties, rule of law, governance, and civil society. Only rule of law and governance would constitute indirect support for the police.

I estimate that in 2004 only two-thirds (71%) of INL expenditures should be classified as direct or indirect police assistance. In making this estimate, I eliminated all spending for crop eradication and control; alternative crop development; regional narcotics training, which focuses on demand reduction among the general population; the civilian police program, which represents the expenses of the State Department's office responsible for funding the recruitment and deployment of U.S. civilian police to international missions;

international organizations; trafficking in persons; "other global crime" initiatives; and program development and support. Descriptions of these programs are available in the texts of the Congressional Budget Justifications. I have counted in my estimate spending for narcotics law-enforcement and interdiction expenditures under the Andean Counterdrug Initiative and selected items for non-narcotics crime control, specifically border security, "anti-crime programs," and support for the four International Law Enforcement Academies. American International Law Enforcement Academies (ILEAs) have been established in Budapest, Hungary; Bangkok, Thailand; Gaborone, Botswana; and Roswell, New Mexico. The latter provides advanced training for graduates from regional ILEAs. Another ILEA is planned for the Latin American region.

I have chosen not to include INL's expenditures for anti-trafficking in people as direct assistance to the police, but instead classify it as indirect assistance (table 3.3) because the program addresses many aspects of the problem outside of law enforcement, such as demand reduction for sex trafficking, developing a sex tourism prevention program, creating a global database on victims, building shelters for victims, and assisting in drafting anti-trafficking laws (INL Budget Justification, FY 2005).

I have included all funding provided by the Foreign Operations budget for anti-terrorism assistance administered by the Department of State. This includes the Antiterrorism Assistance (ATA) program and the Terrorist Interdiction Program (TIP). Both provide money for technical training and equipment to improve the capability of foreign law-enforcement, security, and border protection agencies.

The Foreign Operations budget also appropriates funds for two laws explicitly designed to aid the development of democracy in eastern Europe and the countries of the former Soviet Union, both of which have been exempted from Section 660. They are the FREEDOM Support Act (FSA) of 1992 and the Support for East European Democracy (SEED) Act of 1989.[4] Some of this money is passed along to support law enforcement programs of INL. The FSA money was directly used to assist police forces in the former

---

4. The SEED Act's exemption to 660 is contained in the act itself; the exemption for the FSA is granted annually in the Foreign Operations Appropriation Act, as well as being covered by Sect. 534 of the FAA.

Soviet Union (U.S. Department of State, Office of the Coordinator of U.S. Assistance to Europe and Eurasia 2003). In FY 2003, SEED money supported six INL programs, four of which are listed in table 3.2. The other two—"anti-trafficking" (of persons) and "criminal justice system"—I have included as indirect assistance to the police in table 3.3.

I have also included in table 3.2, but have not counted in my estimate of direct assistance, money provided to the Department of the Treasury and the Department of Defense that can be used for training foreign law-enforcement personnel. I cannot estimate in either case the amount of money spent on police personnel. To do so would require examining the agency affiliations of everyone who participates in their respective training programs. The Treasury Technical Assistance program, for example, which is relatively small, can involve police in connection with training related to money laundering and financial crimes law enforcement. The bigger source of underestimation is the International Military Education and Training (IMET) program administered by the Department of Defense under section 541 of the Foreign Assistance Act. Of particular relevance to this study, it can provide money for training of foreign non-defense personnel either abroad or in the United States in order to enhance "cooperation between military and law enforcement personnel with respect to counternarcotics law enforcement efforts" (FAA, Section 541). In 2003, there were just over ten thousand foreign participants in IMET programs. How many of them may have been police, I cannot tell. However, based on the exhaustive list of overseas training courses conducted by the Department of Defense (DOD) that is jointly provided by the Departments of Defense and State, I conclude that DOD assistance programs that directly impact foreign police are small relative to those of INL (Interagency Working Group 2003).

The Department of Defense has also been authorized by Congress, using its own budgetary appropriation, to train people abroad, some of whom may be civilian law-enforcement personnel. According to fiscal law, unless Congress grants such authorization explicitly, the Department of Defense, or any other federal agency, cannot undertake foreign law-enforcement training. Current programs that might involve civilian training include counterterrorism, counternarcotics, disaster response, and ad hoc programs undertaken by commanders in combat operations coordinated with local American ambassadors (U.S. Department of Defense and U.S. Department of State 2003). These expenditures are not subject to Section 660 restrictions. The largest of these programs by far is for "Counter-Drug Training Support" (CDTS), enacted in 1991 as Section 1004 of the National Defense Authorization Act. This training is limited to military personnel, although it plainly impacts local law-enforcement activities. The Department of Defense also funds a Regional Defense Counterterrorism Fellowship Program. It too is restricted to foreign military personnel, and all candidates are vetted by the local American embassy for human rights violations.

The direct-police table does not include American support for police or any justice assistance carried out by multilateral institutions, which would include the cost of recruiting, training, and deploying U.S. police personnel to UN missions and the percentage cost of UN peacekeeping missions automatically charged to the United States. These costs vary considerably from year to year. Nor does it include American contributions to UN trust funds established for countries in which the United Nations has intervened, donor conferences for societies emerging from conflict, such as Bosnia-Herzegovina, or the United Nations Development Programme, which has a small police-assistance program. In addition, the United States contributes to the World Bank and to the Inter-American Development Bank, both of which provide small amounts of security assistance that sometimes involve law enforcement (Ball 2001; Biebesheimer 1999).

Finally, I have not listed the U.S. Agency for International Development (USAID) as a funder of police assistance because, as a matter of policy since 1975, it does so rarely and on a very limited scale.[5]

Even though I cannot estimate the amount of money involved, I have listed in table 3.3 the major government programs that support the development of democratic institutions abroad and are known to have a justice component. Such programs can have an important but indirect effect on the institutional context in which the police work, thus impacting directly both their effectiveness and their rectitude. The most common justice component involves encouragement of the rule of law and fostering protection of human rights.

5. In 2004, for example, it had only two police projects—in El Salvador and Jamaica.

Because these programs are large and complex, composed of hundreds of sub programs, it is impossible to determine with any reliability how much money is devoted specifically to the justice sector, let alone how much is spent in ways that support democratization of the police. I have, however, indicated allocations for programs that are clearly justice related. These totals provide some sense of the amount of money available for general democracy development and could constitute an important multiplier of the effectiveness of democratic assistance programs focused on the police.

There are other federal organizations that have generic democracy training programs, some of which may have justice components. The Interagency Working Group (IAWG) on U.S. Government-Sponsored International Training and Exchange lists eleven (IAWG 2003).[6] I have not provided budget figures for these programs.

I want to reiterate that $634.6 million is my estimate of the size of civilian, non-secret U.S. government assistance to foreign police. It is inexact, and it does not account for foreign assistance that indirectly affects police development abroad. Considering the number of qualifications that had to be made about this estimate, one might justifiably wonder whether the exercise was worth doing? I think it was. It provides for the first time an order-of-magnitude estimate of police assistance. Let those who can produce better information, throw the first stone. The estimate shows accurately enough that despite the legal prohibition on providing foreign assistance to the police, the U.S. government is doing it in a big way. It also seems reasonably clear that while police assistance may not be the dominant part of democracy programs, it is central to the justice component. Finally, the difficulties I have described in making this estimate show how the entire enterprise lacks transparency. More than once, people in government whom I asked for information indicated politely that they thought I was on a fool's errand. The lack of reliable information about police assistance is frustrating not

6. Department of Defense, Defense Security Cooperation Agency; Department of State, Bureau of East Asian and Pacific Affairs, Bureau of Educational and Cultural Affairs, Bureau of South Asian Affairs, and Office of International Information Programs; Broadcasting Board of Governors; Center for Russian Leadership Development; National Endowment for Democracy; Office of Personnel Management; U.S. Agency for International Development; and the U.S. Institute of Peace.

only to people outside government but also to people inside who know only too well the confusion, duplication, waste, and cross-purposes that beset development efforts in the justice sector. Not only should others try to provide a more accurate tally, but the entire enterprise of police assistance should be subject to systematic accounting as well.

If one were to make a complete inventory of America's role in justice assistance, there is another dimension that ought to be assessed, namely, the support given by the private sector. Liberally estimated, it is possible that private foundations award as much as $17 million to international programs involving crime, justice, and legal services. This is based on the fact that in 2000, according to the Foundation Center, the largest 1,015 American foundations awarded $2.45 billion to international programs, 37% to foreign and 63% to domestic recipients (Foundation Center 2002). Unfortunately, the Foundation Center does not provide a programmatic breakdown of international expenditures. Assuming, however, that the proportion of foreign grants going to foreign recipients for "crime, justice, and legal services" is the same as the proportion going for the same services in domestic programs (1.9%), one arrives at the $17 million figure. Because private foundations do not usually contribute directly to agencies of foreign governments and because of the sensitivity of assisting police in any case, it is doubtful that private American philanthropy is currently making much of a contribution of the development and reform of police abroad. The U.S. government is by far the dominant player with respect to foreign police assistance.

Agencies Providing Assistance

The agencies that are given money to provide assistance to police overseas are not the agencies that may actually implement such programs. The Department of Justice, for example, receives no money from the Foreign Operations Budget to provide overseas training and assistance. At the same time, it is a key agency that does so. In order to understand police as well as justice assistance, a distinction must be made between its funders and its providers.

The agencies that provide, as opposed to fund, non-secret foreign law-enforcement assistance are shown in table 3.4. The biggest player providing "normal assistance," meaning outside of military operations and peacekeeping, is the Department of Justice.

The International Crime Investigative Training and Assistance Program (ICITAP) is the only government institution created specifically to provide foreign assistance directly to the police. It has a peculiar history reflecting the equivocal position of police assistance in current U.S. government policy. ICITAP was created by Congress in 1985 as an explicit exception (Section 534[b][3]) to the Section 660 prohibition. ICITAP, which employs about 40 staff in Washington and overseas, provides development assistance for criminal investigation, basic police training, anti-crime strategizing, management, and democratic values and practices (Call 1997; Stromsem 1997). Most of its work is done through private contactors.

In terms of government organization, ICITAP is an anomaly. It is located within the Criminal Division of the Department of Justice, but its funding comes largely from USAID with supervision by the Bureau of International Narcotics and Law Enforcement Affairs (INL) of the Department of State. In effect, the sole organization in the U.S. government whose statutory purpose is assisting police abroad operates through bureaucratic slight-of-hand rather than by coherent authorization and consistent Congressional oversight (R. M. Perito 2000).

The Department of Justice also provides indirect assistance to law enforcement through the Overseas Prosecutorial Development, Assistance, and Training Program (OPDAT) and the Office of Justice Programs (OJP) of the Department of Justice. OPDAT is funded by both INL and USAID. OJP supports training through its Office of Victims of Crime and the National Institute of Justice.

For reasons explained earlier in the chapter, the U.S. Agency for International Development provides almost no assistance directly to foreign police. During the 1980s and 1990s, almost all of its money for police assistance went through INL to ICITAP (U.S. Agency for International Development 2002).[7] Historically, then, develop-

---

7. Money also flows the other way between these two. On occasion, INL gives money to USAID to provide "administration of justice" programs in support of its counternarcotics and anticrime programs (U.S. Department of State, Bureau of International Narcotics and Law Enforcement Affairs, FY 2003, Congressional Justification).

Table 3.4
Agencies Providing Police Assistance

I. Department of Justice

Antitrust Division: International Technical Assistance Programs
International Criminal Investigation Training Assistance Program (ICITAP)
Overseas Prosecutorial Development and Assistance Training (OPDAT)
Federal Bureau of Investigation (FBI)
Drug Enforcement Administration (DEA)
National Institute of Justice (NIJ): International Programs
Office of Justice Programs (OJP)

II. Department of Treasury

Bureau of Alcohol, Tobacco, and Firearms (BATF): International Training
Program
Federal Law Enforcement Training Center (FLETC):
International Banking and Money Laundering
Training Program; Professional Development
Training Program; Undercover Operations
Training Progam
Internal Revenue Service (IRS): International Programs

III. Department of State

Antiterrorism Training Assistance (ATA)
Terrorism Interdiction Program (TIP)

IV. Department of Defense

Defense Security Cooperation Agency
Defense Threat Reduction Agency
Afghanistan
Iraq

V. Department of Transportation

Coast Guard
Federal Aviation Administration

VI. Others

Department of Commerce, Bureau of Industry and Security (BIS);
Patent and Trademark Office (USPTO)

National Transportation Safety Board
Security and Exchange Commission (SEC)
U.S. Agency for International Development (USAID)
U.S. Postal Services (USPS)
Office of Special Counsel: International Visitors Bureau

VII. Private Contractors

DyneCorps
CACI International Inc.
and others

Source: Interagency Working Group on U.S. Government–Sponsored International
Exchanges and Training 2003.

ment assistance for the police has shifted from USAID in the 1970s
to the Department of State today, which sub-contracts the work to
specialist law-enforcement organizations within the government and
to private contractors.

Worldwide Reach

The U.S. government's assistance to police has risen steadily since
the end of the Cold War in 1990. INL's expenditures, for example,
have grown from $147.7 million in 1993 to $1.2 billion in 2004. ICI-
TAP has increased its budget from $13.4 million in 1990 to $41.3
million in 2003. OPDAT's expenditures have risen correspondingly,
from $700,000 in 1993 to $26.3 million in 2003. These increases,
especially those under the Bush administration, represent a growing
concern with international law enforcement that was independent
of trends with respect to general foreign assistance. Indeed, general
foreign assistance declined from 1990 to 2001, from $8.03 billion to
$7.8 billion.[8]

8. These figures are for total USAID-managed funding, which includes programs jointly managed with the Department of State or appropriated through the
Department of Agriculture. Direct appropriations to USAID rose by 50% from 1990
to 2001, from $2.4 billion to $3.2 billion.

Should the approximately $635 million that the United States provides in support for the police abroad be considered a little or a lot?

Compared to what other countries contribute by way of foreign assistance to the justice sector, it is a lot. Unfortunately, this conclusion is inferential from their outlays for total foreign assistance because most major donors do little better than the United States in being able to provide a consolidated figure for expenditures on foreign assistance to police. Among Great Britain, Canada, Germany, Norway, and Sweden, only Sweden could provide a specific figure for police—it spent $11.3 million on police assistance in 2001 (Swedish National Police Board 2002). Officials in the Japanese International Cooperation Agency estimate that less than one percent of their total foreign assistance budget goes into the omnibus category of "government services," which would mean that $8 million at most could be used to assist law enforcement and criminal justice.

Comparing American outlays for police assistance to gross spending by other countries on foreign aid, U.S. assistance to the justice sector amounts to almost one-half of Norway's total assistance budget in 2001 (Norwegian Agency for International Cooperation 2001), one-third of Japan's (Japan International Cooperation Agency 2001), one-quarter of Australia's and Canada's (Australian Agency for International Development 2002; Canadian International Development Agency 2002), and one-sixth of Sweden's (Swedish National Police Board 2002). It represents 3.0% of Britain's international development assistance in 2002–2003, or slightly more than its proportion of American assistance (Department for International Development 2003).[9]

Actually, the biggest direct contributor to global policing is by far the United Nations. For FY 2002–2003, the United Nations spent just over $2 billion on civilian police operations (United Nations,

9. This comparison understates British foreign assistance because the Foreign and Commonwealth Office also provides money to development and peacekeeping activities abroad. Two programs are directly relevant to police and criminal justice, namely, some of the work of the British Council, budgeted at £147 million in 2001–2002, and peacekeeping, budgeted at zero in 2001–2002 but £133 million the previous year.

Department of Peacekeeping Operations 2003). That is three times more than the United States spent on police assistance in 2003. To be fair, however, part of the UN outlay was contributed by the United States, some in support of the American CIVPOL contingent and some to the UN's peacekeeping and development accounts.

In terms of outreach, American police assistance in some form went to over 150 counties in 2003 (U.S. Department of State, Bureau of International Narcotics and Law Enforcement Affairs 2005). This means that the United States reached out to police in three quarters of the world's countries, offering material and technical assistance. Obviously the amounts of assistance varied considerably, but the range of activity is nonetheless impressive.

One form of assistance—training—can be estimated in reliable detail. In 2002, approximately 30,000 foreigners were trained by the U.S. government agencies primarily involved in providing direct assistance to the police. See table 3.5. At the same time, other agencies have programs that the Interagency Working Group on U.S. Government-Sponsored International Exchanges and Training (IAWG) classifies as serving the national interests of "law enforcement" and "counterterrorism." If they are included (V–VIII, table 3.5), then close to 80,000 foreign people, not exclusively police, were trained by the U.S. government in police-related matters. Much of this training represents what I have called "indirect" assistance to the police. This would be especially true of USAID training, which accounts for the bulk of this category.

The source for this information is the annual report of the IAWG. Created in 1997, the IAWG provides, in its own words, "the only full account of all U.S. Government-sponsored international exchanges and training activities" (IAWG 2003). The inventory for 2002 covers 218 international programs, involving 630,000 participants, and representing an investment of $1.3 billion.

Nature of Assistance Programs

American programs of police assistance are overwhelmingly directed at increasing the law enforcement effectiveness of foreign agencies rather than reforming them according to democratic criteria. The

Table 3.5
Foreign Participants Trained, 2001–2003

	2001	2002	2003
I. Department of Justice			
Antitrust Division: International Technical Assistance Programs	655	180	0
Bureau of Alcohol, Tobacco, and Firearms: International Training Program	643	698	740
ICITAP	2,638	417	35
OPDAT	5,371	5,032	3,462
Visitors Program	801	908	975
FBI	6,594	8,030	5,399
DEA	1,767	2,047	2,247
Office of Justice Programs, National Institute of Justice, International Activities	299	98	122
II. Treasury			
Customs	1361		
III. Department of Homeland Security			
Customs and Border Protection International Visitors			923
International Training and Assistance Program Law Enforcement Training Branch			1,258
International Training and Assistance Program Assistance Projects Branch			1,825
Federal Law Enforcement Training Center (FLETC):	233	64	29
1. International Banking and Money Laundering Training Program	233	64	29
2. Financial Forensic Techniques Training Program			21
3. International Visitors			36
4. International Individual Students			25
5. Interview Training			22
6. Training Needs Assessment-Ukraine			20
Immigration and Customs Enforcement			
1. International Visitors Program			214
2. ICE International Training Program			1,130
International Affairs International Training and Visitor Program			120
Transportation Security Administration			432

IV. Department of State

Anti-Terrorism Assistance	3,908	4,700	5,335

V. Freedom Support Act (FSA)

	6,074	5,868	6,023

VI. Support for East European Democracy (SEED)

	485	719	652

VII. Department of Defense

Defense Security Cooperation Agency: IMET	8,386	10,417	10,736

VIII. Others

Department of Commerce Patent and Trademark Office Technical Assistance Programs	128	960	1,147
Security and Exchange Commission	311	601	
USAID: Democracy and Governance	20,568	34,813	
U.S. Postal Service Training Program	191	1217	

Source: IAWG 2004,

primary purpose of foreign assistance is to make criminal justice agencies in other countries more effective at combating the forms of crime that are considered most threatening to the United States, such as terrorism, illegal narcotics, money-laundering, and trafficking in persons.

This judgment is based on the descriptions of programs provided by major police and justice assistance agencies as well as inventories of international training sponsored by the U.S. government. The vast majority of American programs of assistance to the police involve enhancing foreign capacity to find, arrest, and punish criminals more effectively—for example, by purchasing equipment, especially for communications and transport; creating specialized units; professionalizing management; revising personnel policies; drafting policy manuals; providing protective equipment for individual officers; augmenting forensic skills and equipment; training in criminal investigation, intelligence gathering, and crime analysis; developing training curriculum; drafting strategic plans; and facilitating regional law-enforcement cooperation.

The Bureau of International Narcotics and Law Enforcement Affairs, which provides the bulk of assistance that goes directly to foreign police, provided an informative breakdown of the kinds of its assistance given in 2004 (U.S. Department of State, Bureau of International Narcotics and Law Enforcement Affairs 2005). Fifty-two and a half percent went to crop eradication and narcotics interdiction and 47.5% for "alternative development/institution building." However, very little of the latter went for institutional reform of law-enforcement. Nineteen percent was spent on "alternative development," referring to support for economic activities not involving narcotics cultivation; 15.3% on anti-crime programs; 3.3% on border control; 2.2% on program development and support; 1.2% on international organizations; 1.0% on trafficking in persons; and 0.2% on the "civilian police program," meaning administrative costs of recruiting and deploying U.S. civilian police to international missions." Only 4% of the INL budget went for "administration of justice and support for democracy."

It is unclear how much of that was spent on police reform as opposed to revision of laws, changing other sectors of the criminal justice system, and public education. For example, INL spent 1.2% of its budget on training in its four International Law Enforcement Academies where, according to their advertising, human rights and rule of law are "woven throughout the fabric of the program." In fact, the "Human Dignity Course" taught by personnel from the John Jay College of Criminal Justice in New York City accounts for only two to three days of the eight-week course. At the Budapest ILEA, it has been reduced to one day, including an hour-long presentation on the differences between U.S. and European legal systems and reports by foreign participants on the organization of their police.

Although all American assistance programs to the police stress the need for the observance of human rights and promotion of accountability, the fact is that few of them do so directly. The exceptions are those that improve internal discipline by setting up internal investigative units in police or prosecutorial organizations; develop capacity to investigate violations of human rights; encourage formation of special offices to prosecute official corruption; improve access to courts; create external monitoring agencies; and provide training in the rule-of-law and ethical law enforcement. Most of these are provided by programs of indirect rather than direct assistance to the police.

Terminology can be misleading in categorizing programs, and descriptions that sound reformist may not be. Many rule of law programs clearly contribute to law-enforcement capacity building, for example, developing anti-kidnapping strategies, pursuing follow-up investigations of financial crimes, creating a bomb squad/explosives database, instituting prison security and drug rehabilitation training, and developing cellular police communications. INL's rule of law project in Colombia in 2003 included "continuing support for the Colombia National Police to reestablish public security in the rural areas, strengthening the planning and management capability of the civilian Ministry of Defense, and encouraging members of the illegal armed groups to leave the battlefield and be reinserted into society" (U.S. Department of State, Bureau of International Narcotics and Law Enforcement Affairs 2003). In its study of American rule of law programs from 1993–98, the General Accounting Office (GAO) estimated that 57% went to criminal justice and law enforcement, 21.3% to judicial and court operations, 13.6% to civil government and military reform, 6.3% to democracy and human rights, 1.5% to other, and 0.3% to law reform (1999). This confirms a conclusion it had reached in an earlier study that most programs of American law enforcement agencies train foreign police to meet American law enforcement needs (U.S. General Accounting Office 1993).

In his study of American foreign assistance, Thomas Carothers concludes that most programs conducted by American law-enforcement agencies have "an uncertain and sometimes contradictory relation to democracy goals" (1999b). ICITAP is the exception to this pattern because it was created to enhance foreign criminal investigations skills so as to investigate human rights abuses more effectively, especially in Central America.

Looking at all international training and exchange programs in 2002 supported by the U.S. government, the Department of State's Interagency Working Group found that of 218 programs, 38% served U.S. national security interests (regional stability, counterterrorism, and weapons of mass destruction), 34% democracy and human rights, and 23% law enforcement (Interagency Working Group 2002). "Law enforcement" was defined as minimizing the impact of international crime and reducing the flow of illegal drugs. Clearly law enforcement in the sense of building capacity abroad is a major emphasis of American foreign training. Considering that few of the democracy and human rights programs focus on the police directly because of the section 660 prohibition, it is fair to say that direct assistance training to police is dominated by capacity building rather than normative reform.

Conclusion

American efforts to assist police forces abroad are substantial, costing about $635 million per year in 2004, touching three-fourths of the world's countries, and directly involving several thousand police officers and other justice officials. Most assistance is directed at developing the law-enforcement and crime-control capabilities of foreign police. Very little serves to facilitate police reform directly. Indeed, a great deal of assistance that would seem democracy facilitating, such as rule of law programs, actually build capacity that can be used in any way local governments decide.

The function of providing foreign police assistance is concentrated in a handful of U.S. government agencies and the funding for it is monopolized by one—the Bureau of International Narcotics and Law Enforcement Affairs of the Department of State. USAID, which is the designated instrument of American foreign assistance, plays hardly any role. Even though responsibility for assistance to police abroad is relatively concentrated, it is not directed by clear legislative intent. Instead, police assistance is undertaken under the cover of exemptions made to a legislative prohibition against assistance to foreign police at all. As a result, American development aid to foreign police is provided in an ad hoc way responding by and large to concerns about criminal threats to the United States rather than to the goal of expanding democratic criminal justice practices.

4

Strategies of Reform

In order to achieve democratic reform in police agencies, what programs of foreign assistance should be provided? How can the international community, both bilaterally and multilaterally, facilitate the institutionalization of democratic policing? International experience suggests, I believe, six substantive programs that are critically important.

1. Provide a legal basis for the new police.
2. Create specialized, independent oversight of the police.
3. Staff the police with the right sort of people.
4. Develop the capacity of police executives to manage reform.
5. Make the prevention of crime as it affects individuals the primary focus of policing.
6. Require legality and fairness in all actions.

These courses of action do not exhaust all the useful things that might be done to assist countries engaged in peaceful regime change or emerging from conflict. They are the programs that are essential to furthering *democratic* reform. In other words, if foreign assistance does not do these things, it will not achieve democratic reform.

In addition, I shall argue that three assistance programs commonly thought to facilitate democratic police reform are not essential to reform and, in fact, divert attention from more important activities. These are (1) organizational restructuring, (2) material support, and (3) generalized training.

The key to determining the kind of programs foreign assistance should support in order to bring about democratic police reform is the development of a plausible theory specifying the way in which the actions proposed connect to the goals to be achieved. Unfortunately, such explicit thinking is rare in planning foreign assistance (U.S General Accounting Office 2001). Programs are commonly developed and funded on "a wish and a prayer," without a clearly articulated and factually informed justification for what is proposed. In the case of democratic police reform, the goals to be achieved are adherence by police to rules of law embodying internationally recognized human rights, acceptance of external oversight, and responsiveness to the community (chapter 2).

Ideally, a validating theory would be based on experience in similar situations showing whether particular forms of assistance really did, on balance, produced stipulated reforms. For reasons that will be discussed in chapter 7, such evidence at the moment is weak. Consequently, the recommendations made here will not be based on systematic evaluation but on the informed opinion of practitioners and observers of police reform.

The order in which the recommendations are presented does not reflect their importance for achieving democratic reform. The great difficulty of reform is that many things need to be done at the same time. Like building a masonry arch, all the stones need to be place before it can bear weight. At the same time, the list reflects a rough chronological priority in implementation. Some programs require others to precede them. The sequencing of these steps are set forth in an algorithm of reform at the end of the chapter.

Programs Essential to Reform

1. *Provide a Legal Basis for the New Police*

Reform cannot occur if there is no agreement on, and consequently legal authorization for, the form that policing will take in a reformed government (Call and Stanley 1999; Neild 1999; Stromsem and Trincillito 2003). There must be a legal blueprint that provides for those features of policing bearing most directly on adherence to the rule of law and human rights, on external accountability, and on implementing community-responsive strategies. Legal authorization would specify the mission and functions of the police, their powers, the institutions of external oversight, internal disciplinary mechanisms and standards, responsibility for appointing and promoting personnel, and sources of funding.

In two countries, El Salvador and South Africa, international assistance made a major contribution to this goal. The interim government in El Salvador between 1991 and 1994, acting on general agreements about policing provided in the Chapultepec Accords that ended the civil war, enacted, with the assistance of foreign advisors, a new police law, penal code, and code of criminal procedure (Chinchilla 2001). Similarly in South Africa, a detailed plan for police reform was developed prior to the election of Nelson Mandela and the African National Congress in 1994. One feature was the requirement that government set up "community-police forums" in every police station (Brogden 2002; Marks 2002). This was later incorporated into the 1996 constitution.

Such agreements on authorization did not occur during the establishment of new governments emerging from conflict in Panama (1990), Cambodia (1991), Somalia (1992), Bosnia-Herzegovina (1995), and Iraq (2003). In Bosnia-Herzegovina, for example, the Dayton Accords that ended the conflict (December 1995) failed to provide any guidance about the form that policing should take. The United Nations International Police Task Force (IPTF) deployed in early 1996 immediately developed its own principles for democratic policing, subsequently expanding them into the *Commissioner's Guidance for Democratic Policing in the Federation of Bosnia-Herzegovina* (1996). Unfortunately, the *Commissioner's Guidance* was never fully implemented. Its recommendations were resisted by politicians in all the "entities" created by the Dayton Accords — the Serb Republic, the Bosnian-Croatian Federation, and many of the cantons within the Federation (International Crisis Group 2002). Furthermore, the recommendations were never consistently implemented by the United Nations Mission in Bosnia-Herzegovina. By 2000, few members of the IPTF had heard of it, and copies of it were difficult to find either in Sarajevo or New York.

Providing a fundamental police law is especially problematic in peacekeeping situations where there is no legitimate government. Peacekeepers are in the delicate position of advocating democratic self-government while imposing, sometimes unilaterally, a law that determines the way in which security and order, the basic responsibilities of any government, will be shaped and regulated (Hartz and Mercean 2003).

2. Create Specialized, Independent Oversight of the Police

Reforming governments must create effective oversight over the police (Clegg, Hunt, and Whetton 2000). Incorporated ideally into the new police law, oversight must be part of the vision for a democratic police force. External oversight needs to be independent of government control, guaranteed adequate funding, and exclusive in its focus on police. Its oversight should cover two aspects of police performance: (1) effectiveness in achieving public safety and (2) fairness in operational behavior.

A detailed model for such oversight has been developed by the Independent Commission on Policing for Northern Ireland, known as the Patten Commission (1999). It recommended creation of two bodies to ensure police accountability, namely, a Policing Board to oversee strategic direction and performance and an Ombudsman to receive and investigate complaints about improper and illegal conduct. According to the reports of the Oversight Commissioner created to oversee the transition to a new police, both institutions have taken hold and performed with thoroughness and professionalism (Oversight Commission 2001–2005). The renamed Police Service of Northern Ireland has accepted both institutions with good will and worked cooperatively with them.

Efforts to create effective external oversight were not successful in either El Salvador or Bosnia-Herzegovina. In El Salvador the National Council on Public Security created in 1996 never performed, but became an advisory body to government on social crime-prevention. In Bosnia-Herzegovina, the recommended "Independent Police Inspection and Review Agency" was never created (Monk 2001).

It is advisable to create two oversight agencies, as the Patten Commission suggested, because the functions of ensuring accountability of the police for both effectiveness and fairness are respectively very complex, requiring different processes of evaluation and different assessment skills. In addition, the functions may contaminate one another. For example, controversy generated by the investigation and reporting of misbehavior may undermine the willingness of the police to participate in assessments of their effectiveness.

Holding the police to account for the way in which they perform their duties, as opposed to their effectiveness in doing so, should be designed to prevent misbehavior in two distinguishable ways: (1) by evaluating patterns of abuse and recommending corrective legal/ administrative action, and (2) by deterring indiscipline through the investigation and punishment of individuals who misbehave. Too often, institutions of external oversight are viewed exclusively as deterrent devices. This is a mistake. In addition to investigating and punishing erring officers, it is important for them to analyze patterns of misbehavior and to suggest administrative remedies. For example, the federal government in the United States has begun requiring police agencies with records of abuse to create "early warning systems" by which to collect information about the activities of officers in order to determine whether they are at risk for misbehavior (Independent Commission on the Los Angeles Police Department 1991; U.S. Department of Justice 2001). Such officers are then retrained, reassigned, or counseled.

Because the deterrent function of investigating and punishing officers has historically been monopolized by the police, they bitterly resist, everywhere in the world, any encroachment on it by nonpolice. Recently, however, civilian oversight agencies in many of the world's developed democracies have been given authority to investigate alleged misbehavior and, more rarely, to impose punishment (Walker 2001). With respect to both investigating and disciplining, the powers given vary substantially across jurisdictions. They include (1) reviewing the adequacy of responses by the police, (2) directing the police to take particular actions, and (3) superceding police authority altogether and substituting their own independent judgment (Bayley 1996b).

In order to make oversight successful in holding police to account for discipline, however, it is also essential to make the registration of complaints easy and not intimidating. Moreover, in order for complaints to be specific enough to be acted on, police officers must be identifiable individually during the performance of their duties (Independent Commission on Policing for Northern Ireland 1999). They should be required to wear nametags or identity numbers.

3. Staff the Police with the Right Sort of People

Whether democratic reform follows the overthrow of authoritarian governments by its own people or the imposition of international peacekeeping after conflict, the old police will have been discredited. In all likelihood, they will be distrusted and feared by the populace. It is essential, therefore, that the attitudes and behavior of police officers, especially those at senior levels, be changed. At the same time, however, there are undoubtedly pressing problems of public safety that need to be addressed. A country cannot declare a "time out" on crime and disorder while the police get their attitudes adjusted. In peacekeeping situations the international community may temporarily take responsibility for law and order, although military peacekeepers are reluctant to do so because they are not properly equipped or trained to perform police duties (Perito 2003).

There are two solutions to the staffing dilemma: (1) disband the local police and quickly recruit again or (2) retain existing staff and change their outlook and practices. The closest any country has come recently to creating a totally new police was El Salvador, which disbanded the entire security establishment—army, police, and rural civil defense groups—after 1991. The more common pattern is for selective purging to be combined with retraining of old personnel and rapid recruitment of new. Although the effect on safety and security from such disbanding is unclear, and often politically controversial, there is no doubt that efficiency and discipline suffer. The paradox is that because the selective discharge of personnel—"vetting"—falls most heavily on senior and therefore more experienced officers, the police may lose the capacity to undertake their own reform (Martinez and Amaya 2000). For example, Poland dismissed

all high-ranking officers after the collapse of Communism (Haber-
feld 1997). Because experienced junior officers were then promoted
too quickly, six Chief Commanders had to be removed within five
years, badly tarnishing the reputation of the new police. In one
case, an officer who had been a captain in rural area in charge of
twenty-two police officers rose within a few months to become a
Chief Commander in charge of 100,000. Similar problems occurred
in East Germany where the Federal Republic refused to employ any
former Stazi officers after reunification in 1990 (Harlan 1997).

Despite the obvious desirability of excluding people with
records of human rights abuses from the ranks of the reform police,
selective vetting is often difficult. The United Nations mission in
Bosnia-Herzegovina, which had full powers to reconstitute the local
police, worked for seven years (1996–2002) to produce a certified list
of officers who did not have criminal records, were not guilty of war
crimes, and had not occupied the houses of refugees (Monk 2001;
United Nations Mission in Bosnia and Herzegovina 2002; International Crisis Group 2002).

Selective purging of tainted personnel is also difficult when
it is undertaken by newly constituted, reformed governments, as
in El Salvador, Haiti, and Guatemala, because it may be perceived
as favoring the followers of one group of former combatants over
another (Stromsem and Trincellito 2003; Neild 1995, 1998b). Selective purging threatens hard-won political agreements about the
composition of the new police, as in Kosovo where 50–55% of police
officers were to be from the Kosovo Liberation Army (KLA) or as
in El Salvador where 30% were to be from the former government,
30% from the rebels, and 40% new recruits (Hartz and Mercean
2003). Allegations about political favoritism arise as well with promotions of junior officers to positions vacated by discredited commanders (Human Rights Watch 1997). In El Salvador, the United
Nations discovered that the new government presented ineligible
candidates for recruitment from the former army, National Guard,
and Treasury Police (Stanley 1996b). The same was true of the commission of colonels appointed by President Aristide in Haiti in 1995
(Neild 1995).

It is generally agreed that if some "rolling over" of old personnel into a new police service is necessary, it should involve individuals and not entire units. Units retain an internal cohesiveness

that is more resistant to reform and more likely to perpetuate old habits (Stanley 1996b). It is also not a good idea to resort to the expedience of recruiting from the military into the police, at least not without extensive retraining. This is particularly true for senior officers who, although they may have had useful command experience, bring a style of leadership as well as orientation toward the public that is generally not conducive to democratic reform. There may, on the other hand, be substantial benefits in recruiting experienced civilian managers to senior positions because they may be more collegial in style, more at ease with external oversight, and more sympathetic to public input (Byrne, Stanley, and Garst 2000; Bayley and Skolnick 1986).

In sum, staffing the police with the right sort of people involves making difficult judgments about the heinousness of previous behavior, the current needs of law enforcement, the balance of political interests, the prospects for reform in the police, and the importance of the police achieving legitimacy in the eyes of the public. While the lessons about what to avoid have become obvious, doing so in particular situations is not subject to easy prescription.

4. Develop the Capacity of Senior Officers to Manage Reform

There is universal agreement among observers of police reform that sustained and committed leadership by top management, especially the chief uniformed officer, is required to produce any important organizational change. Reform does not start at the bottom and percolate upwards. Reform is managed into existence by people who have the power to direct and shape organizations (Bayley and Skolnick 1986; Boydstun and Sherry 1975; Burgreen and McPherson 1990; Couper and Lobitz 1991; Goldstein 1990, 1993; M. Moore 1997; Sparrow, Moore, and Kennedy 1990; Wilson and Walsh 1997; Toch 1980). Senior officers must ensure conformity between the behavior of personnel and the reform goals envisioned. This cannot be brought about by command; it is achieved by time-consuming, labor-intensive persuasion through each level of the organization (Couper and Lobitz 1991; Kelling and Brattan 1993; Stephens 1994; Oettmeier and Brown 1988; President's Commission on Law Enforcement and Administration of Justice 1967; White and Gillice 1977). Nor can it be brought about by simply changing personnel in key positions. Managing reform requires, fundamentally, the ability to recognize how leverage can be exerted through an organization and then ensuring that it is done.

In general, successful efforts to change police organizations proceed through the following steps. It begins with the recognition by the senior commander, or group of senior officers, that change is needed. The development of a specific plan for change that draws on the experience of all ranks and specialties within the organization is then worked out by a small group of officers working directly with the senior commander. Practical plans for implementation are then developed through consultation throughout the agency. These plans are selectively implemented to test their viability and evaluated for their success. Finally, the reform program is adopted and implemented throughout the organization.

The essential lesson is that management itself much be transformed. In most police agencies this means changing from a directive, top-down, quasi-military style to a participatory, bottom-up, collegial style (Bayley and Skolnick 1986; Kelling and Bratton 1993; Stephens 1994,). It also requires more than raising the technical level of management. Reform requires adopting a mind-set that puts a premium on judging itself by the demonstrable achievement of objectives. Adopting this mind-set is the primary way that the objective of being effective in crime control, the primary rationale for police, can be squared with the obligation to be humane, with which effectiveness often seems in conflict. The logic of this will be discussed at length in chapter 5.

If the key to reform is management, what are some of the actions that police commanders may take? I suggest the following:

- Supervise subordinate managers closely to ensure that they are not half-hearted or willfully subversive in their support of reform.
- Remove from positions of responsibility officers who are not committed to reform.
- Provide resources for pilot projects designed to test whether particular programs lead to desired reforms.
- Solicit reactions from subordinates who are implementing new approaches and revise plans as necessary.
- Assist officers to learn from one another about how new approaches can more successfully achieve old objectives.

- Develop and adapt policy manuals, job descriptions, and performance indicators to reflect reform objectives.
- Incorporate an understanding of the reform vision into the training for all personnel—recruits, in-service officers, and civilian employees.
- Reward responsive officers with commendations, promotions, and opportunities to teach others.
- Assign new recruits to cutting-edge reform activities so they may learn first-hand what the organization is trying to achieve.
- Re-design uniforms, flags, insignia, and badges to indicate to police officers and the public alike that a significant change is being made.

5. Make the Prevention of Crime as It Affects Individuals the Primary Focus of Policing

Being responsive to the safety needs of individuals is one of the defining elements of democratic police reform (chapter 2). In order to do this, the priorities of the police must shift from "national security" to "serving and protecting." Three programs are especially important in bringing about this reorientation.

First: Police must consult with the public to determine what safety-related problems trouble them most. This is the centerpiece of "community-oriented policing," which became the most popular reform movement of the late 20th century. Under this rubric, police in many countries have encouraged the creation of community groups with which they meet on a regular basis. Northern Ireland, for example, now requires "consultative forums" in the areas patrolled by each community police officer. It has also created "District Police Partnerships" in its political sub-divisions, composed of almost equal numbers of politicians and non-elected members of the public (Independent Commission on Policing for Northern Ireland 1999). Similarly, South Africa began its "transformation" of policing with the development of Community Police Forums in 1995 (Department for International Development 2003; Van der Spuy 1999).

Through consultative groups like these, police discover that their priorities often differ from those of the public. For example, crimes such as murder, assault, housebreaking, and robbery may not concern the public nearly as much as behavior that is more disorderly than seriously criminal, such as rudeness toward women in public places, rowdy teenagers congregating on street corners, begging and drunkenness, traffic hazards for school children, and willful destruction of community property (Bayley 1994; Goldstein 1990; Skogan 1990; Skogan and Frydl 2004). Police learn then, if they are truly listening, that public respect and support depends on addressing less dramatic forms of disorder than they have customarily done. Moreover, that they must develop new ways of measuring success, ways which depend less on statistics and more on narrative accounts of problems solved to the satisfaction of communities.

At the same time, being responsive does not mean that the police do exactly what people want. Police powers are limited by law, as well as by resources, and the public may want the police to do unacceptable things, such as torturing suspects for confessions, enlisting them in private vendettas, harassing people regarded as undesirable, turning a blind eye to unlawful activity, and covering up vigilante excesses. Civil society, which so many foreign assistance programs want to strengthen, may not be very civil.

Although consultation between police and the public is a key part of developing responsiveness, it may become a thinly disguised mechanism for spying and surveillance, especially in countries with authoritarian traditions. Rather than adapting strategies to local needs, police may use consultative institutions for control and intelligence gathering (Bayley 1994; Call 1999a; Caparini and Marenin 2003). Consultation becomes not a genuine interchange of views but an exercise in cooptation. Even in democratic countries, police often see responsiveness primarily as a public-relations tool for mobilizing the public for its purposes rather than obtaining a more informed sense of what they should be doing. For this reason, community policing has been oversold as a device for achieving democratic law-enforcement. It is not a universal prescription for democratic policing.

Second: Police must demonstrate that when members of the public seek help, they will be treated promptly, sensitively, fairly, and effectively. The most dramatic improvement in police responsiveness occurred with the creation of emergency telephone-radio dispatch systems in the early 20th century (911 in the United States, 110 in Japan, 999 in Great Britain). By this means individuals, no matter their status, can summon authoritative assistance to stop disorder and provide immediate relief to distress (Bayley 1994). This sort of individually responsive police service is still rare in the world. Its implementation would revolutionize the relation between police and public in many countries and substantially increase the legitimacy of the police.

Third: As part of becoming responsive, police must make it easier, more convenient, and more comfortable for individuals to solicit their help. This can be done in a variety of ways:

- By refurbishing the reception areas of police stations so the public has easy access to police staff as well as comfortable places to wait.
- By assigning officers to patrol on foot or bicycle so that they are more approachable than when patrolling by motor vehicle.
- By sympathetically listening to complaints and providing immediate action or referral.
- By courteously explaining the reasons for their actions, especially when they stop motor vehicles or question people on the street.
- By training telephone operators to listen, diagnose, and explain courteously and professionally.

In Bosnia-Herzegovina, for example, the U.S. International Criminal Investigation Training Assistance Program (ICITAP) provided bicycles to the police so that people in Sarajevo could contact them more easily. ICITAP also provided a costume for "Safety Bear," a police officer who visited schools and neighborhoods to teach children about crime prevention and traffic safety. This proved vastly popular, and was a dramatic demonstration of the new orientation of the former-Yugoslavian police.

6. Require Legality and Fairness

Creating effective disciplinary systems within the police, along with oversight outside the police, should be a first-order priority in democratic reform (Byrne, Stanley, and Garst 2000; Call and Stanley 1999; Neild 1998b; Stromsem and Trincellito 2003). Indeed, some observers advocate this as a condition for continued foreign assistance (Stanley 1996a). ICITAP, for example, was instrumental in creating a Professional Standards Unit in the Bosnian-Croatian

Federation and the Serbian Republic that developed regulations for investigating allegations of misbehavior (International Crisis Group 2002). Creating effective "internal affairs" units is sensitive everywhere, but it becomes doubly controversial in countries emerging from conflict where the personnel composition of the police has become politicized.

But deterrent discipline is not enough. It must be accompanied by educational programs that stress the norms of lawfulness, human rights, and individual dignity, so that officers do not receive tacit approval for law breaking, abuse, and corruption. Education in these norms can occur in a variety of ways.

- Develop, adopt, and publicize statements about the values that police actions should serve.
- Hold ceremonies at which officers publicly swear to abide by the law and the values of the organization.
- Enact concise codes of ethics to replace the usual lengthy and detailed disciplinary regulations (Independent Commission on Policing for Northern Ireland 1999; Marks 2002).
- Provide training in ethics that involves illustrations from the rough-and-tumble of active service (Marks 2002).
- Develop clear statements of policy about the handling of problematic events, such as the use of firearms or high-speed motor-vehicle chases.
- Most important of all, commanders and supervisors must stress the importance of legal, courteous, and professional conduct at all times. They must reinforce this message informally at ceremonies, roll calls, inductions of new members to their units, and in casual conversations. They must be eternally alert for wrongdoing, and must not only invoke formal sanctions, such as suspension, demotion, or forfeiting pay, but also softer ones like retraining, reassignment, and uncompromising mentoring.

Programs Not Essential to Reform

There are three programs of assistance that are widely considered to make important, even essential, contributions to democratic reform.

They are reorganizing, equipping, and training. Faith in these programs is misplaced. None of them is a prerequisite for democratic reform, although each may make a contribution if implemented on the basis of a local assessment of needs. When these programs are applied generically, as all-purpose inputs regardless of the stages of reform or local conditions, they divert and mislead.

1. *Reorganizing*

Changing police behavior, which is the key to democratic reform, will not occur by reorganization of police agencies. Democratic policing is not a set of structures but a set of practices. It is compatible with a variety of organizational structures. This observation applies whether one is talking about changing the internal organization of the police or its national structure. National structures, in particular, coincide with historical distributions of power and change very slowly over time (Bayley 1975; Bayley 1985). Moreover, there is no necessary connection between democracy and any particular mode of organization or control over the police. The best evidence for this is that the organization of policing varies considerable among the world's democracies. Democratic countries may have decentralized police (the United States) or centralized ones (France), a single national police (Sweden) or multiple national police (Italy), close political supervision (United States) or remote political supervision (Japan), constitutional limitations on police power (Canada) or statutory ones (Great Britain), and combined or separate police organizations for preventive as opposed to investigatory policing (United States/France).

Police advisors often act on the presumption that democratic policing requires the structure they are familiar with at home. This explains why advisors from different democratic countries give conflicting advice about structural reform. American advisors, for instance, tend to recommend decentralization as a prerequisite for democratic policing. But they mistake cause for effect. Countries aren't democratic because they have decentralized police; they have decentralized police because they are democratic (Bayley 1985). Thomas Carothers makes the point very nicely:

> Unconsciously or consciously, many American confuse the forms of democracy with the concept of democracy. There is

an unfortunate combination of hubristic belief that America's ways are the most democratic in the world and lack of knowledge about life in other democratic countries. (1999a)

The lesson for police reform is that new bottles don't make new wine. Changing the table of organization does not change attitudes and mind-sets. Reorganization is also likely to exhaust the reform impulse as people fight about the reorganization itself, leaving little enthusiasm for more fundamental changes.

2. Equipping

Providing material resources such as cars, weapons, and radios may encourage democratic reform, but it is never sufficient and rarely essential to bringing it about (Sismanidis 1997; Stanley 1993, 1996a).

The Japanese government, for example, donated a very expensive and sophisticated automated fingerprint identification system (AFIS) to El Salvador in the 1990s. It was never used. The United States gave 2000 vehicles to the El Salvador police, but half of them were quickly wrecked or damaged by personnel who had never driven before. This prompted ICITAP belatedly to train several police employees in vehicle repair and maintenance. European governments have donated equipment for DNA analysis throughout southern Africa only to find it wasted by police who lacked the basic skills of criminal investigation (Department for International Development 2002).

Stories like these are not rare; they are told in every country where police assistance has been given. It's only fair to note, however, that police in developed countries also often put the technological cart before the operational horse. Providing microcomputers to British police officers, for example, did not lead automatically to problem-solving analysis until management provided access to usable databases and the incentives to use them (Chatterton 1993). In general, investments in information technology (IT) have not led to more intelligent and far-sighted policy-making until managers recognized the need for it and acquired the skills to use it (Manning 1992). The point to stress is that physical resources make no contribution to reform, whether normative or operational, unless they are used and sustained in that usage for the ends intended.

There are, on the other hand, some cases where the material needs of the police are so urgent that it is unrealistic to expect improvement, let alone reform, without critical inputs. When the United States and the United Nations intervened in Haiti in 1995, they discovered that the local police lacked uniforms, handcuffs, radios, and even doors, windows, and roofs for police stations (Neild 1996, 1998). In Bosnia-Herzegovina in 1996, the United Nations International Police Task Force tried to encourage democratic practices among police officers that did not have belts to hold up their trousers. Unfortunately, too much foreign assistance is provided not to make up for such fundamental deficiencies but because the local police want the "bells and whistles" that are associated with sophisticated policing, or because foreign advisors can't imagine working without them.

Although raising the technical level of foreign police does not automatically produce democratic reform—indeed, it may simply empower repression—material and technical assistance may be the price that foreign reformers must pay to obtain and sustain commitment to reform (Blair and Larsen 1994; Royal Canadian Mounted Police 2003). Determining the nature as well as the amount of assistance involves negotiation, particularly when foreign donors have an explicit agenda, such as democratic reform. Furthermore, foreign recipients must be encouraged to "buy into" reform programs for them to succeed. In these circumstances, material resources may be regarded as a "transaction cost" for achieving reform. This is a slippery slope, however, and may lead to substantial imbalance between investments of resources relative to the gains produced. A sounder policy is to provide material assistance only to defray the operational costs of reform for which there is local commitment rather than to using it to induce commitment among people who are otherwise unwilling.

Providing material foreign assistance may also impose additional costs on the recipients that donors should be sensitive to. Local police officials in many countries complain about the complexity of accounting rules imposed by donors. The rules of the European Union, for example, are considered especially complex. Local administrators often do not have the capacity to monitor procurement and expenditures as donors require. As a result, donated funds are not expended as called for or go entirely unused. Because donors want to ensure, justifiably, that assistance is used as intended, donors need to consider whether they should help to defray these administrative costs, perhaps allocating a fixed proportion of grants to building the local capacity to manage them in a sound and transparent manner.

Once again, the lesson is that providing material assistance looks easy, but it works only when managed effectively in terms of specified operational objectives. Ideally, developing the capacity to use assistance should precede the delivery of material foreign assistance. It should at least accompany it.

3. Training

Training is undoubtedly the largest component of foreign assistance programs. Unfortunately, training of new personnel and the retraining of old are not sufficient to bring about reform. The benefits of any training, whether to enhance skills or to change normative orientations, are lost if opportunities are not immediately provided for people to apply what they have learned (Boisvert, Menard, and Ostiguy 2000; Call 1997; Cohen and Wheeler 1997; Interagency Working Group 1998; Marenin 1999; Mastrofski 1999). Learning must be reinforced by practice on the job.

In order for training to make a difference to reform, it must "be provided at the right moment, be tailored to the job, and must carry real consequences" (Marks 2002). In other words, it should be given when it is needed to the people who can use it immediately. Borrowing a practice from modern industry, training for police should be provided "just in time," not warehoused in the brains of people for that remote day when they might use it. By implication, training should not be given as a reward to favored officers, to people on the verge of retirement, or to people who are likely to be promoted or reassigned to other work.

It also follows that the best training that foreign advisors can give will be on the job where they can demonstrate in operational terms how to think and work like a democratic cop.

Conclusion

The essential ingredient in developing successful programs of foreign assistance is the explicit articulation of the linkages between assistance inputs and reform objectives. It is not good enough to assume an impact. Its likelihood must be demonstrated either from experience or through an explicit and plausible description of the operational connection. The substantive programs that I have recommended for achieving the four defining elements of democratic policing are summarized in figure 4.1.

The algorithm in figure 4.1 shows what foreign assistance should be focused on in order to achieve democratic reform. Even though each step will be implemented roughly in the sequence suggested, they must all be foreseen from the outset. Investment in the enactment of laws requiring the police to observe international standards of human rights, for example, may be lost if the police are unwilling or unable to investigate misbehavior. Training new police officers may not change the culture of the organization if management lacks the skill to employ them in ways that utilize that training. And every investment is jeopardized if managers throughout the organization fail to translate democratic prescriptions into operational practice.

Designing assistance programs to implement each of the steps outlined is complex, requiring informed delivery and local knowledge. There is specialized writing about all of them and knowledgeable experts to implement them. My recommendations are where planning begins, not where it ends.

There is a final and very important point to make about reforming police. Police reform will fail unless the rest of the criminal justice system changes at the same time. Criminal justice reform is seamless and it cannot focus on one justice sector to the exclusion of others. Reform must address the entire "intelligence-to-incarceration continuum," and the interlocking needs of the police, prosecutors, judges and court administrators, and prison officers (Hartz and Mercean 2003). For example, it does little good to train police in the collection of physical evidence if judges regard confessions as the sine qua non for conviction. This lesson has become commonplace in writing about justice assistance. It is often neglected in practice, however, not just because it adds to the cost and complexity of reform but because governments that provide justice assistance are rarely organized to take a holistic view. Instead, justice assistance is spread among various agencies, each specializing in a different sector of criminal justice.

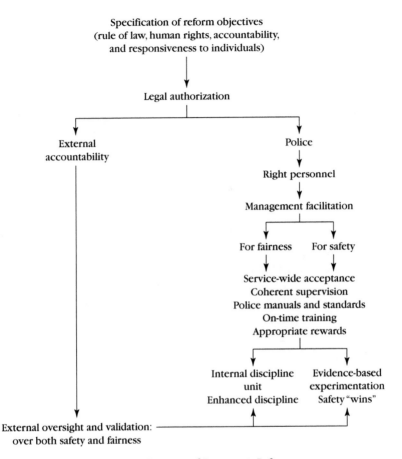

Figure 4.1 Programs of Democratic Reform

Designing a reform program is a daunting task, requiring an intimate knowledge of the workings of police organizations, strategies of management, connections of police to larger criminal justice processes, and the historical practices of criminal justice wherever reform is undertaken.

5

Security and Reform

The reform of police institutions in order to support the growth of political democracy is always impeded and sometimes wholly undermined by threats to security. Increases in crime, terrorism, violent public demonstrations, or guerilla insurgency shift political agendas from reform to enhancing security (Bayley 2001; Byrne, Stanley, and Garst 2000; Carothers 1999a; Goldsmith 1997; Koci 1998; Marenin 1998; Popkin 1999; Schmidl 1998). In political life, the requirements of security trump aspirations to reform, a pattern to be found in stable as well as struggling democracies. As a consequence, foreign donors find themselves under enormous pressure to retard, amend, or stop programs of reform assistance.

The operational question for the international community is whether foreign assistance to the justice sector can achieve democratic reform in the face of growing insecurity. Must the needs of law-enforcement take precedence over the requirements of institutional reform?

I do not believe so. While it is certainly true that governments, including democratic governments, require stability and order, it is not true that democratic reform is an obstacle to the achievement of that. On the contrary, democratic reform of the police increases rather than undermines the ability of government to protect itself and the public.

This chapter will explore the relationship between security and reform and its implications for assistance policies. The discussion will, first, describe the nature of security threats that reforming countries face; second, explore the contribution that security makes to democracy and that democracy makes to security; and, third, recommend principles that should guide justice sector assistance in order to achieve both reform and security.

The Security Challenge

The threats to security that challenge reform are twofold—violence directed against the state and crime affecting the general population. The former is generally conducted by groups, the latter generally by individuals. The threats to government come in the form of terrorism, mass demonstrations, violent strikes, widespread civil disobedience, guerilla insurgency, or organized military attacks. Terrorism by dissident political elements is particularly difficult to deal with, as the British discovered with the Irish Republican Army (IRA) in Northern Ireland, the Spanish with Basque separatists, Israelis with Hamas and Hezbullah, and the Sinhalese in Sri Lanka with the Tamil Tigers. In post-conflict situations especially, arms are plentiful and former combatants are unemployed, habituated to violence, and bitter.

The second threat to security comes from increases in crime against the general population. The causes are many: demobilized combatants, widespread unemployment, prolonged absence of effective policing, discredited institutions of justice, growth of organized crime, loss of informal social control by families and communities traumatized by conflict, easy access to weapons, and the growth of vigilantism (Call 2003; Call and Stanley 1999; A. S. Hansen 2002; United Nations 2001). It is often difficult to document such increases with reliable data. Members of the public are reluctant to report crime to discredited police agencies and governments lack the administrative capacity to tabulate them. Furthermore, crime reporting itself becomes politicized, with hard-liners exaggerating the threat and reformers minimizing it. What is indisputable, however, is the almost universal perception wherever new democratic governments are established that public safety is at risk. This was true, for example, in South Africa, El Salvador, Bosnia-Herzegovina, Hungary, Czechoslovakia, Russia, and the other former Soviet republics following their respective efforts to create reformed governments during the 1990s. A survey by the World Bank found that after a decade of democratic reform in Latin America people were as concerned about personal safety as about unemployment and poverty (Brock and Chambers 2001). The survey also discovered that criminal victimization correlated with support for authoritarian solutions, summary justice, and military government.

Perceptions of a "security gap" following political transitions are common both in countries that are emerging from conflict, as in Bosnia or Afghanistan, and in countries that are reforming peacefully, as in Poland or Russia. The power of this perception is enormous. Governments cannot ignore threats to their own survival, nor, if they want to develop their democratic bona fides, can they fail to respond to the fear of crime felt by the general populace (Bayley 1975, 1985). This imperative has several effects. Government's attention as well as physical resources will be shifted from institutional reform to security effectiveness. Police agencies will become more centralized, hierarchical command intensified, more lethal weaponry deployed, operations conducted more commonly in groups, and force used more often. Police agencies will also claim greater latitude in operations, becoming more independent and less accountable to external supervision. If governments face politically inspired violence, they will give priority to protecting themselves, shifting resources from general crime prevention. In these circumstances, the military is more likely to be given, or to recover, a domestic law-enforcement role and police, conversely, to operate in a more militaristic fashion (Bayley 2001; Schmidl 1998).

But it is more than just conditions inside countries that push governments to emphasize law enforcement over reform. Foreign providers of police assistance often give priority to law-enforcement capacity building rather than institutional reform (Bayley 2001; Call 1999a, 1999b; Diamond 1995). They are prompted to do this, even when they have a genuine attachment to democratic policing, for several reasons.

First: Their own security needs. During the Cold War a major goal of American foreign policy was to enlist allies in resisting Communism. Today a major goal is to develop collaborative relations with other countries against criminal threats such as terrorism, the importation of illegal drugs, money laundering, and trafficking in people (Call and Stanley 1999; Huggins 1998; Nadelman 1997; Snow 1997; Stanley and Lossle 1998). As was demonstrated in chapter 3, most of America's security-sector foreign assistance goes to enhancing the capacity of law enforcement. And it is implemented largely by federal law-enforcement agencies. The International Law Enforcement Academies (ILEAs) that the United States has established in Hungary, Thailand, and Botswana are modeled on the FBI Academy at Quantico, Virginia, and are designed to upgrade the skills of people in operational law-enforcement agencies and to enlist their cooperation in international crime control ventures.

Second: Diplomatic convenience. Because donors and recipients often share an interest in effective crime control, enhancing skills and providing equipment serves a common agenda. Reform, on the other hand, imposes norms that may be regarded as a foreign imposition and is therefore more likely to be resisted. Diplomatically it is easier to offer gifts than to insist on change. For this reason, reform is regarded by donors as political, therefore controversial; capacity building as technical, therefore politically neutral.

Third: Influence. Justice assistance is sometimes provided to ensure donor presence, both politically and commercially, rather than to produce reform. Capacity building serves this agenda very well by synchronizing security strategies between donor and recipient and providing markets for entrepreneurs (Blair and Lansen 1994).

Ironically, the human rights community, both local and foreign, may also advocate capacity building rather than reform in order to improve the ability of the police to investigate human rights violations both retrospectively and prospectively. When governments change, criminal investigation may serve the process of reconciliation by bringing the perpetrators of past abuses to justice, as in Northern Ireland or South Africa (Popkin 1999; United Nations, Department of Peacekeeping Operations 1999). America's International Criminal Investigation Training Assistance Program (ICITAP), for example, was set up largely to assist Central American countries to investigate more effectively the alleged atrocities committed by guerilla groups. Prospectively as well, capable investigation is required to make the police accountable for their own behavior, a feature of democratic policing.

Altogether, then, many interests—public safety, governmental stability, international criminality, foreign policy, persistent abuses of human rights—coalesce to shift development agendas from democratic reform to more effective law enforcement. The security agenda is powerful in its champions and powerful in its effects. Meeting the security concerns of both local and foreign constituencies, therefore, is essential if reform is to be achieved.

False Choice

Must governmental security and public safety be bought at the cost of democratic development? That is the usual assumption. It is false. Providing safety and achieving democratic reform should not be seen as antithetical goals. Democratic reform cannot occur without an essential minimum of security. Conversely, however, democratic reform can make the achievement of security more likely. Let's examine both of these assertions.

Democratic reform requires effective security, hence attention to the law-enforcement capabilities of government, for five reasons.

1. *Safety for individuals in their person and property is itself a human right.* The essential function of government is protection of its people from external as well as internal threats. Simply as a matter of definition, "government" implies a minimal amount of public order. The opposite of government is anarchy. Providing safety is essential, therefore, for legitimacy. As Van Creveld says, "The most important single demand that any political community must meet is the demand for protection" (1991). One can, therefore, make a strictly utilitarian argument that without security, people are unlikely to support reform (Gray and Manwaring 1998; Neild 1996; Washington Office on Latin America and the American University School of International Service 1990).

If safety is a human right in the sense of being a fundamental obligation on any government, then shouldn't law enforcement effectiveness be included as one of the characteristics to be achieved in the democratic reform of police, in addition to the rule of law, human rights, accountability, and responsiveness to individuals? I don't think so. Creating order by itself isn't democratizing. Order is a condition for democratic reform, but ordering can be achieved at the expense of democracy. There is an asymmetry in the relationship between security and democracy. Order can be achieved without democracy, as happens in prisons, but democracy cannot be achieved without minimal order. Providing satisfactory safety is a desired consequence of policing in a democracy; it is not a defining characteristic of democracy.

2. *Democratic processes require the rule of law and the rule of law requires an effective champion.* That champion is the state. The hallmark of democracy is commonly considered to be the holding of free and fair elections. The United States has promoted this as the litmus test for democratic government abroad. But free and fair elections require, in turn, defense of key civil rights, the most important being the right to free speech, publication, association, assembly, and movement (Bayley 1964). This implies legal guarantees that are effectively enforced. Especially in societies riven by violence and mistrust, factions need a referee who is both strong and impartial (Kaplan 1998; Woodward 1995). That is the function of government, and especially of its primary executive arm.

We are accustomed to thinking that democracy is the means for achieving human rights. While this is correct, it overlooks the fact that without minimal guarantees of human rights, democracy cannot be achieved. This is the real paradox underlying the tension between security and reform. Democracy requires the privileges that are promised by its creation. As Fareed Zakharia has argued, elections constructed without providing for fundamental civil rights lead to the creation of "illiberal democracies" (Zakharia 2001). Or, as a UN publication put it, "[O]ne multiparty election does not a democracy make" (United Nations 2002a).

3. *All governments, even democratic ones, have enemies, some of them willing to use force.* This is especially true for governments emerging from prolonged civil strife or governments dedicated explicitly to social changes. Consequently, proponents of democratic reform must be willing to assess the seriousness of politically moti-

vated threats and to join with government in developing effective methods for dealing with them.

4. *Democratic accountability requires the police to have the capacity to identify, investigate, and discipline abusers of human rights, both among themselves and elsewhere in society.* Failing to develop effective law-enforcement skills not only leaves the public unprotected, it undermines the ability of the community to hold the police accountable as well.

5. *Research has shown that economic development is a facilitator of and perhaps even a prerequisite for democracy* (Department for International Development 2000; Leggett 2001; USAID 2002). At the same time, economic development requires, in turn, minimal security and order. Crime has long been recognized as both the result and the partial cause of economic deprivation (Braithwaite 1989; Currie 1985). This proposition is now well accepted by international development agencies such as the World Bank, the International Monetary Fund (IMF), and the Inter-American Development Bank (IDB), as well as by bilateral contributors such as USAID, the United Kingdom's Department for International Development (DFID), and the Canadian International Development Agency (CIDA).

In sum, foreign assistance that aids the development of the law-enforcement capacities in reforming states should not be viewed reflexively as part of a sinister, reactionary plot. Providing public safety serves the interests of democracy.

The converse proposition, however, that democratic practices by police enhance the capacity of states to provide security is more controversial. Police and the public generally think that democratic reform is synonymous with being "soft on crime." They fail to recognize that democratic reform can powerfully assist in the process of creating a safe society.

What is the evidence for this proposition?

1. *Knowledge about crime comes primarily from the public.* Police don't discover crime; they are told about it by victims (Skogan and Frydl 2003). They are led to it by members of the public willing to do so. People who are alienated from the police conceal criminality, believing that they have more to lose by bringing it to the attention of the authorities than by remaining silent.

Being able to obtain accurate knowledge about the nature and extent of crime and disorder from the public is essential for developing and implementing effective public safety strategies. Furthermore, neither tough nor soft crime policies can be assessed for their effectiveness without reliable data on the amount of it to compare police efforts against. Police officials and politicians are only pretending to be serious about public safety if they have not done all in their power to encourage the public reporting of crime.

2. *The crimes that people fear most, such as homicide, assault, rape, robbery, burglary, and theft, are rarely solved without information supplied by the public that identifies the likely perpetrator.* Research in the United States and Great Britain shows that without public input the police can solve only about 10% of cases (Greenwood, Petersilia, and Chaiken 1977; Skogan and Frydl 2003). In popular fiction, detectives collect facts that lead them to perpetrators. In the real world, the public identifies likely suspects and detectives collect information that proves these suspicions to be true. Then arrests can be made that will lead to successful criminal prosecution.

Information provided by the public is also crucial to the success of investigations designed to prevent, disrupt, and deter crimes that harm society as a whole, such as terrorism, illegal drug dealing, and trafficking in people. These might be called "macro" crimes because, although they harm individuals, they are not directed at particular individuals. To use military terminology, in macro crimes individuals are "collateral damage" in the criminal enterprise. The preferred strategy of most police agencies against macro crime is to create specialist undercover squads to penetrate such conspiracies in order to prevent future occurrences and prosecute offenders. It has long been recognized, however, that a public willing to provide information about suspicious people and activity not only deprives "macro criminals" of a place to hide but also provides information that allows the police to target their proactive operations. This has been shown to be true in quelling guerilla insurgencies as well as in deterring terrorism and narcotics trafficking (Kissinger 1965; Komer 1975; Thompson 1969). In law enforcement there is no substitute for a cooperative public, whether against macro or micro forms of criminality.

3. *Because the numbers of police are limited and they cannot be a deterrent presence everywhere, effective crime control requires the public to take actions that prevent crime.* The public must become co-produc-

ers of safety. They do this by watching for and reporting dangerous situations and persons, patrolling public places under the supervision of the police, and guarding one another's property. The populace at large can also do something the police can't: It can maintain social discipline, especially with respect to the young, by teaching, admonishing, praising, and punishing. Ordinary people have more influence over would-be deviants than the criminal justice system ever does (Bayley 1994; Nagin 1998).

4. *Research has shown that people are more likely to obey the law when its practitioners have treated them with fairness* (Braithwaite and Braithwaite 1995; Sherman et al. 1998; Tyler 1990). The behavior of law-enforcement authorities, quite apart from the formal sanctions they administer, affects positively and negatively whether people will accept law. Respectful treatment increases compliance; disrespectful treatment decreases it.

Police themselves know this, as when they advise one another not to arrest men in front of their children, not to humiliate people by having them kneel on the ground, or not to use disrespectful (or exaggeratedly respectful) language to members of disadvantaged groups.

Furthermore, the perception that the police commonly behave in arbitrary and inconsiderate ways increases the suspicion between police and public, thereby raising the likelihood that their activities will be met with anger and violence. This generates a reinforcing cycle of greater police control, increases in abuse, heightened public fear, sullen disrespect, violent resistance, and more control (Kamisar 1964; Kelling and Coles 1996).

5. *Persistent police abuse of human rights diverts attention and resources from controlling criminals to controlling the police* (Bayley 2002). Costly criminal and civil prosecutions against police increase, and contentious and time-consuming efforts are made to create independent oversight of the police. These efforts depress the morale of the police and generate a defensive us-versus-them mentality. This further undermines the ability of the police to make common cause with the public against criminal activities.

In sum, democratic reform of the police enhances their ability to prevent and control crime by mobilizing the public in its own defense, encouraging the sharing of information with the police that is essential to measuring and preventing crime, building the legitimacy of law, concentrating resources on crime-fighting rather than misbehavior prevention, and developing the necessary self-esteem of the police that is the prerequisite for dedicated performance.

Contrary to what many police, politicians, and members of the public think, violation of democratic practices hampers rather than helps the creation of the order and safety that people so deeply desire. In the words of the Independent Commission on Policing in Northern Ireland (Patten Commission), set up after the Good Friday Agreement of April 1998:

> We cannot emphasize too strongly that human rights are not an impediment to effective policing but are, on the contrary, vital to its achievement. Bad application and promiscuous use of powers to limit a person's human rights—by such means as arrest, stop and search, house searches—can lead to bad police relations with entire neighbourhoods, thereby rendering effective policing of those neighbourhoods impossible. (1999)

Squaring the Circle

Accepting the proposition that effective law enforcement is an essential ingredient of democracy and the further proposition that democratic practices by police enhance law-enforcement effectiveness, what should programs of foreign assistance to the justice sector do in order to pursue both harmoniously? I recommend seven principles of action.

1. *Priority should be given to developing the capacity of police forces to manage by results.* In order to serve their publics both more effectively and more humanely, police need to be able to think strategically about their goals and tactics. This is rare. Most police forces in the world, even in many donor countries, do not have reliable information about what they are doing, let alone what they are achieving. They manage by anecdote, myth, and gut instinct, clinging to strategies that have never been shown to be effective. The plain fact is that most of the policies that constitute being "tough on crime" have never been shown to work. The common presumption that demo-

cratic reform inhibits effective crime prevention is a myth founded on ignorance.

Foreign police, and many donor police as well, need to develop what has become known as "evidence-based policing." They must develop a managerial mind-set that insists that evidence be provided to show that what the police propose to do is likely to have the intended effect. The best example of this is New York City's celebrated CompStat (computer statistics) system that requires commanders to demonstrate that the strategies they are following accomplish the crime-control goals of the organization (McDonald 2002). If they cannot, commanders are told to formulate new plans, based on the best available thinking, and return to the CompStat forum to defend them. However, the key to CompStat, despite the name, is not the technology; it is the system of management accountability based on timely analysis of results.

What are the hallmarks of evidence-based decision making in a police agency? How would one determine whether a police agency knows what it is doing? I suggest the following six-question test.

1. Can the police demonstrate that their primary crime prevention strategies are making a difference?
2. Have they evaluated current operational programs against others?
3. Are they currently conducting any controlled experiments in policing strategies?
4. Does senior management routinely discuss alternative approaches to crime prevention?
5. Are police personnel assigned and deployed according to evidence that doing so enhances effectiveness?
6. Can police demonstrate the reliability of the information they have about their own activities and the results of them?

If a police agency can't answer these questions affirmatively, then there is little hope that it can become effective at crime control.

In addition to making the police more effective with respect to their core responsibility, the development of an evidence-based mind-set serves other important functions at well. First, it provides the information that can make the police accountable—one of the elements of democratic reform. Accountability cannot be imposed on the police from outside if the police are not accountable to themselves. If police do not have current and accurate information about the activities of their personnel, it is extremely unlikely that people outside will have any better.

Second, an evidence-based mind-set is also essential in order to correct the view common among police that deferring to human rights—another element of democratic policing—undermines their law-enforcement effectiveness, especially their ability to catch and prosecute criminals and thus deter future criminality. This may sometimes be true, but more often is not. Moreover, if it is true sometimes, it is essential that the precise circumstances in which the violation of rights may be useful must be specified so that guidance may be given to police officers and support obtained from the public.

The message underlying this recommendation is that foreign advisors should be very careful not to advocate or encourage crime-control strategies abroad that haven't been shown to work at home. The developed democracies, notably the United States, Great Britain, Canada, and Australia, have learned a great deal from research about what works (Sherman 1998; Skogan and Frydl 2004). The most important are the following:

- Deterrence through the criminal justice system is not the solution to crime. Crime rates are overwhelmingly a function of socioeconomic factors such as unemployment, school achievement, poverty, income inequality, residential mobility, and households headed by single women (Braithwaiate 1989; Cohen, Felson, and Land 1983; Currie 1985; Sampson 1987; Skogan 1990; Walker 1989).
- Police strategies applied generally rather than being targeted on particular persons, places, and situations, are unlikely to be effective.
- Increasing the number of police beyond minimal levels does not deter crime nor reduce the fear of it.
- Reducing the time in which police respond to reports that crimes have been committed neither increases the likelihood that the criminal will be caught nor satisfies the public with the police response.
- Focusing police activity on resolving conditions underlying recurrent problems that generate fear in the public and

repeated calls for police attention are much more effective at reducing crime and the fear of crime than treating every incident as a singular event.

Saying that these lessons have been established by solidly grounded scientific research does not mean that they have been widely accepted as the basis for crime policy. Sadly, these lessons are often unappreciated in the very countries that have studied them most extensively.

It follows that assistance designed to build law-enforcement capacity should not be given unless that capacity is to be used as part of an explicit and defensible crime-control strategy. Capacity building is not an end in itself. It must be appropriate for the particular needs of each country and justifiable in terms of "best practices" around the world.

Finally, capacity building should not be focused on technology but rather on the skills required for strategic management (Clegg, Hunt, and Whetton 2000). Failure to do this explains why so much technical assistance is ineffectively used or wasted altogether.

2. *Offers of foreign assistance should be contingent on local police implementing the four specified democratic reforms: rule of law, human rights, accountability, and responsiveness.* If a police force does not take meaningful steps to adopt these practices, assistance programs should be terminated, and not on the normative argument that these practices are essential to democracy but the narrower one that democratic reform will increase law-enforcement effectiveness by encouraging the public to become co-producers of public safety (Trojanowicz and Bucqueroux 1990). How do each of the essential practices of democratic policing—rule of law, adherence to human rights, external accountability, and responsiveness—contribute to law-enforcement effectiveness?

Insistence on following the rule of law reduces arbitrariness in law enforcement, enhancing its perceived fairness and thereby encourages allegiance to it.

Human rights provide the substance of the rule of law. Without them, the rule of law, while not arbitrary, could be cruel, biased, and repressive, resulting in a hostile and alienated populace.

Accountability is a mechanism not only for assessing the rectitude of police behavior but also for determining whether the police are being effective in their primary responsibility, namely, protecting society. Accountability is the keystone to both effectiveness and reform.

Finally, responsiveness to the needs of individuals has two advantages for crime control: it reduces the tendency for police to become "regime police," focusing exclusively on the needs of government, and it demonstrates to an often-skeptical public that government is on their side (Bayley 1985).

As a corollary to the principle that foreign assistance should not collude in supporting undemocratic practices, people who provide foreign assistance must never accept the notion that focusing on technical capacity-building is less political than pressing for institutional reform (Carothers 1999b). Everything that is done with the police is political in the sense that it supports one rather than another agenda, shifts power among factions within the police, and affects the relations of people to government. To be responsible in providing assistance, foreign donors must accept that there are political consequences to whatever they do.

3. *Foreign assistance should be given primarily for addressing the security needs articulated by individuals rather than those articulated by governments.* At the very least, assistance in support of government security should not be at the expense of concern for the safety of individuals.

The distinction between government security and public safety is not as neat as this principle implies. All unlawful activity harms individuals, whether through ordinary crime, macro crime, or subversion of political processes. The problem is that fighting subversion and macro crimes diverts attention away from the personal security needs of individuals. In the process, individual citizens are transformed from clients-to-be-served into objects-to-be-controlled. Foreign donors must be careful not to accede to this change in focus, especially because the macro crime agenda often fits so neatly with the priorities of the donors (Boisvert, Menard, and Ostiguy 2000).

4. *Countries that provide assistance to foreign police should place local security needs, especially those of the general population, ahead of their own.* Using foreign assistance as an inducement to participate in collaborative international law-enforcement activities has two undesirable consequences for the development of an effective democratic police force. It shifts local resources, which are likely to be scarce, to

programs that primarily benefit donors, and it reduces the attention that will be given to the security needs articulated by individuals. In these ways, it reinforces the tendency of police agencies to serve the agenda of government rather than that of private individuals.

5. *Police assistance directed at reform should create demonstrable crime-control "wins" as rapidly as possible.* Because the siren song of "getting tough on crime" is so powerful, police need to show that public safety can be provided because of, not despite, democratic reform. Promises must be kept, but the promises must also not be too grand. Being successful at crime control does not mean eliminating it, but keeping crime within tolerable levels as locally perceived (Hansen 2002). Experience also shows that "wins" cannot be achieved against all forms of crime at the same time everywhere. Crime-control efforts must be targeted at particular forms of crime in particular places. This suggests that democratic crime control strategies should be undertaken as distinct pilot projects, mobilizing required resources, coordinating police and non-police inputs, and carefully monitoring implementation (Boisvert, Menard, and Ostiguy 2000).

Demonstrable success is also important for maintaining the momentum of reform among the police themselves (A. S. Hansen 2002; Marcotta 1999; Neild 1999). They too must be convinced that democratic reforms will not undermine effective law enforcement. Police are practical people, and they will change if they perceive it to be in their professional interest to do so (Bayley 2002).

6. *Foreign assistance should be used to encourage local police to concentrate their crime prevention and control efforts on their country's poor.* As research consistently shows, the crime that most people fear emanates by and large from slums. The most effective way to reduce it, therefore, is to improve the material well being of the poor. This in turn, however, requires providing security within disadvantaged communities in order to encourage employment, investment, and entrepreneurial activity. Because poor people live closer to the brink of destitution, crime threatens their economic prospects more than it does more affluent people (United Nations Development Program 2002).

Furthermore, because crime control efforts inevitably focus on areas where the poor live, the poor bear the brunt of law enforcement and are apt to be alienated most from the law. Democratic police reforms can have a greater impact, therefore, upon their quality of life and their attitudes toward authority than upon the life and attitudes of the more privileged. In democracies, where numbers count, servicing the needs of the poor may make a major contribution toward the legitimacy of new democratic governments, in addition to providing substantial crime-control benefits.

7. *The police cannot become effective, nor transform their image, if the rest of the criminal justice system remains unreconstructed.* Providers of foreign assistance must not focus on one justice sector to the exclusion of others. They must have system-wide programs of assistance encompassing police, prosecutors, judges, and corrections officials. This lesson has become commonplace in writing about justice assistance, but is often neglected in practice because of the cost and complexity involved.

Conclusion

In order for foreign assistance to contribute to democratic police reform, the security needs of both government and the general populace must be taken seriously. Efforts at reform that neglect the central purpose of the police will fail. On the other hand, reform is not the enemy of effective crime control, despite what police and others may think. Sacrificing reform—in particular, the rule of law, human rights, accountability, and responsiveness—for effectiveness is not a smart choice. Effective crime control and democratic reform are not trade-offs.

Transcending this false choice in practice will not be easy. Evidence for the utility of democratic practices for crime control has only recently been developed. People are prepared to believe that being "tough on crime" requires harsh punishments, forceful law enforcement, restricted procedural protections for accused persons, and greater police autonomy. Furthermore, the police cannot ignore demands for law enforcement on the excuse that they are engaged in democratic reform. Reforming the police is like asking the crew of an airplane to redesign its mechanical systems in the middle of a trans-oceanic flight. Police must be effective and reform at the same time. This is a genuine dilemma that reformers, on one hand, must not dismiss and police officers, on the other, must not solve through traditional nostrums.

Finally, reformers outside police organizations are often not prepared to make the kind of arguments for reform that police are likely to accept. Knowing too well the misdeeds of the police, they tend to view police concerns about crime as excuses for maintaining the status quo. They are not practiced in making common cause with the police in developing effective as well as humane policing. They are habituated to treating the police as adversaries. The solution, I believe, is for reformers to join forces with the police in creating the capacity, both managerially and technically, to evaluate the effectiveness of what the police do. Donors will find it easier to sell reform to foreign police by tying it to progressive professionalism rather than to a normative vision such as democracy. Evidence-based policing is the surest way to develop the breath of vision within the police that resists simplistic solutions and recognizes the benefits of democratic reform for the achievement of public safety.

6

Managing Assistance

In providing assistance to facilitate the development of democratic policing abroad, there must be both strategic vision and tactical skill. The preceding two chapters discussed the former, specifying the substantive programs that will make the greatest contribution to the creation of democratic police. In this chapter, I will examine the tactics of managing reform assistance. I will specify how the providers of foreign assistance should manage assistance so that its strategic democratic elements are more likely to be accepted and incorporated into local police practice.

In my judgment, managers of assistance to the police must do the following seven things in order to be successful in institutionalizing democratic practices.

1. Develop a comprehensive plan.
2. Prepare for the long haul.
3. Adapt reform plans to local conditions.

4. Persuade local stakeholders to support reform.
5. Treat aid recipients as partners.
6. Coordinate assistance efforts.
7. Send the right people into the field.

The Tactics of Democratic Assistance

1. Develop a Comprehensive Plan

Facilitating the development of democratic practices among police abroad is a complex business. As we saw in chapter 4, it requires a careful analysis of the dynamics of development based on a nuanced understanding of democracy. Success does not occur by chance. To raise the prospects of success, an assistance plan should be based on an explicit rationale—a theory—linking assistance inputs to desired outcomes (Stromsem 2000; Wulf 2000). Planning is also essential in order to ensure proper sequencing of assistance efforts (Costa 1995; Gray and Manwaring 1998; Thomas and Spataro 1998). Everything cannot be done at once, and one assistance element may be the prerequisite for another. Finally, because democratic reform is a long-term undertaking, the full costs need to be estimated. Half-hearted, short-term assistance efforts may look progressive and feel good, but they are a waste of time and resources.

Although developing a specific, rationalized business plan should always be a requirement for foreign democratic assistance programs, it is not always possible to do so. This is particularly true when unanticipated humanitarian emergencies arise that require law-and-order assistance, as in Bosnia-Herzegovina in 1995 and East Timor in 2000 (Perito 2003; United Nations Development Programme 2001). The international peacekeeping record in this regard is mixed. The American-led UN-authorized intervention in Haiti in 1995 involved a year of careful planning between the United States and Canada primarily, including a rehearsal of the civil-military command structure (Stromsem and Trincellito 2003). In Kosovo, too, planning for reconstruction under the UN mission (UNMIK) occurred in major donor capitals before NATO bombing ended, based in part on information provided by the advance party of Kosovo Force (KFOR). According to Jock Covey, principal deputy special representative to the secretary general in Kosovo, 80% of the advance plan for civil administration held up on the ground (Covey 2003). In addition, the Organization for Security and Co-operation in Europe (OSCE) sent in a team to survey conditions before international intervention and to develop a "concept" for a reconstituted police (Hartz and Mercean 2003).

The Dayton Accords for Bosnia-Herzegovina (1995), on the other hand, provided neither plan nor powers for post-conflict reconstruction of the civilian police, despite the fact that Annex 11 called for the creation of "effective civilian law enforcement agencies." With commendable foresight, Peter Fitzgerald, the first commissioner of the UN's International Police Task Force (IPTF), and his staff immediately developed detailed "guidance" for the creation of a democratic police force, based on seven principles of democratic policing.[1] Unfortunately, this report was never implemented. Indeed, the plan was entirely forgotten as the IPTF's mission was redefined almost yearly (Interviews in Bosnia 2002; Swedish National Police Board 2000; United Nations Development Programme 2001). Finally, a mission implementation plan for the IPTF was adopted in 2000 that involved setting quotas for the number of police in different parts of Bosnia-Herzegovina (BiH), creating an all-BiH border security agency, certifying that personnel had not committed war crimes or had criminal records, de-politicizing police management, enhancing accountability over the behavior of officers, and installing community-oriented policing (International Crisis Group 2002).

Careful advanced planning also did not take place for reconstruction in East Timor in 2000. UNCIVPOL formulated its mission plan on the spot, inventing a doctrine of "community-based policing service" out of the disparate approaches of personnel from 41 countries (Mobekk 2002).

Although the United States learned in Panama in 1989 (Perito 2002) that advanced planning for law-enforcement and civil administration was an essential part of military intervention and applied this lesson in Haiti in 1994, it failed to do so in either Afghanistan in 2001 or in Iraq in 2003. This failure can perhaps be excused in the case of Afghanistan where immediate military action to deprive terrorists of a haven for training and mobilization was thought to be necessary to prevent further attacks on the United States after 9/11.

---

1. See chapter 1.

This was not the case in Iraq, however, where the need for invasion was foreseen, even if the timing was unclear. The U.S. government singularly, some would say willfully, failed to take measures to provide for public safety immediately following military pacification and to develop local law-enforcement capacity (Perito 2004). Because peacekeeping interventions or preemptive interventions against perceived "threats" are likely to recur, both the United Nations and the United States need to develop generic doctrine for the construction of effective democratic policing and criminal justice by local authorities (Swedish National Police Board 2000; U.S. Institute of Peace 2001; United Nations 2000). This will be easier for the United States than for the United Nations. Although UN police operations, following the recommendations of the Panel on UN Peace Operations (Brahimi Report 2000), have been given the same status within the United Nations administrative hierarchy as military operations, UNCIVPOL lacks the staff and resources to plan and coordinate post-conflict reconstruction (Crosette 2000; Lewis, Marks, and Perito 2002; Scheye 2002). The United States, however, does have the knowledge and resources to formulate such plans. The fact that it has not done so to date reflects a lack of political will and direction, especially with regard to coordinating responsibilities among departments and agencies.

2. *Prepare for the Long Haul*

There is universal agreement among scholars as well as foreign assistance practitioners that democratic reform takes a long time—five years at least, more likely ten or more (Bentley and Oakley 1995; Call 1997; McHugh 1994; Neild 2002; Oakley, Dziedzic, and Goldberg 1998; Perito 2002; Pirnie 1998; Popkin 1999). Germany and Japan are the most successful examples of directed democratic police reform in the recent past. Yet observers agree that it wasn't until the 1960s, almost twenty years after World War II, that the spirit of democratic policing as opposed to its form became institutionalized in practice in both countries (Bayley 1991, 1997). It took the Singapore police about seven years (1982–1989) to shift from a British, vehicle-based response model of operation to a Japanese neighborhood-based crime-prevention model (Bayley 1989). In the United States, the adoption of community-policing since its advent in the 1980s has been fitful, uneven, and lacking in coherence despite being widely accepted in principle and supported generously by the Community-Oriented Police Service Office of the U.S. government (Bayley 1994; Eck and Maguire 2000; Skogan and Frydl 2004).

To have any hope of success, assistance for the democratic reform of policing must be provided long enough to allow evaluation of the achievement of intermediate goals and for mid-course corrections (Biebesheimer 1999). Even the customary three-year cycle of most U.S. foreign assistance is too short because the first year is preoccupied with starting up and the last with closing down (Carothers 1999b). Development of effective local police by the United Nations has been hampered by the uncertainty of financial support from the ad hoc coalitions of countries supporting reconstruction in different cases. It has been an "unsteady stream" at best (Scheye 2002). In short, democratic development requires "stamina" on the part of donors that is altogether too rare, and, indeed, may be unrealistic to expect (Wulf 2000).

Democratic police development in the context of peacekeeping encounters special problems of extending commitment. The development of effective indigenous policing of any character in post-conflict situations almost inevitably requires a continued military presence. Although initial military pacification may happen quickly, military forces may still be needed in order to provide a continuing deterrent presence. Indefinite deployments of military units, however, are unpopular in most countries not only with the public but also with military commanders who worry that "garrison duty" disperses capacity and weakens fitness. Furthermore, there may also be intense local pressure for the foreigners to leave, arising out of a feeling of "resentful dependence" (Fallows 2004). This creates a dilemma for foreign assisters. Their continued presence may be necessary to ensure political stability. In 1996 President Clinton promised that American troops would be out of Bosnia in one year. They are still there. They are still in Kosovo six years after intervention and in Afghanistan four years after intervention. At the same time, their continued presence may undermine the capacity, as well as the willingness, of local people to govern themselves, which is a critical goal in any post-conflict reconstruction.

On the other hand, announcing "exit" dates, popular though it will be both at home and abroad, may be unwise. First, it is very difficult to predict when the military can safely transfer responsibility for security entirely to civilian control. To do so requires assessing future political dynamics, resistance to the new order, likely public-order problems, and public acceptance of the new police. Furthermore, setting exit dates may embolden local people to stifle reform or return to violence (Warner 2000). People bent on obstruction have even less incentive to cooperate if they know that the peacekeepers will be leaving soon.

Is the choice in peacekeeping, then, between staying indefinitely and not intervening at all? Perhaps. Premature withdrawal of assistance may indeed jeopardize the stated objectives of peacekeeping intervention and assistance (Hirsh and Oakley 1995; Sismanidis 1997). Certainly the early announcement of dates for leaving is naive and often counter-productive. Michael Ignatieff is right when he claims that "national interests cannot be secured over the long term by people always looking for the exit" (2002). On the other hand, stopping civil wars and crimes against humanity and alleviating acute human suffering are worthy undertakings in themselves even if future political stability is uncertain. It may be shortsighted but not irresponsible to invade militarily, pacify, and then pull out without contributing to the reconstruction of effective and humane government. In all post-conflict interventions the international community should, however, formulate a plan and estimate the cost of an effective program of sustained democratic reconstruction. This would constitute a baseline against which the likely effects of early withdrawal could be assessed.

3. Adapt Reform Plans to Local Conditions

To produce democratic reform abroad, programs of police assistance must be based on a thorough understanding of the host-country's customs in policing (Biebesheimer 1999; Call and Stanley 1999; Clegg, Hunt, and Whetton 2000; Commission on Post-Conflict Reconstruction 2003; Gregory 1996; Scheye 2002; Wedel 1998; Wilson and Walsh 1999). Tradition imposes habits on people that may impede democratic change, even when the change is recognized as desirable. Necessary adaptations to local practice need to be foreseen to prevent surprises in implementation that cause delay, expensive mid-course corrections, frustration among providers and recipients, and disillusionment with the entire process. One reason that reform takes so long is that it often requires changing mind-sets across many stakeholders, including police, politicians, prosecutors, judges, civic organizations, the media, and the public at large.

Providers of foreign assistance often treat local police as a *tabla raza*, as if reform was a matter of importing interchangeable parts. Donor countries often offer an array of "cookie cutter" courses, particularly on technical subjects, without regard to the qualifications of local personnel, customary practices, supporting infrastructure, or resource sustainability (Goldsmith 1995; Gregory 1996; Hilderbrand and Grindle 1997; Konz 1999; Oakley, Dziedzic, and Goldberg 1998; Stromsem 2000; Van der Spuy 1999; Wilson and Walsh 1997). In 1996, the International Police Task Force in Bosnia-Herzegovina announced an ambitious scheme for democratic reform, including community policing, despite having almost no information about the prewar crime-control strategies of the police. Community policing in Uganda, which was supported by assistance from the British police, was not adopted in the early 1990s because the most important crimes in rural areas were livestock theft, grazing rights, and land disputes, all matters reflecting an absence of community solidarity (Neild 1999).

Understandably, donors recommend programs that have worked for them at home. But while some foreign practices will fit foreign contexts, others will not. Americans, for example, tend to advocate the decentralization of policing, along with community policing and CompStat; Japanese recommend creating fixed neighborhood police posts called *koban*; the Spanish advocate deployment of uniformed officers to fixed locations.

Granting that successful assistance requires adaptation to local conditions, what precisely must be known in order to prepare adequately? As a Bosnian chief of police said to me, "Everything." That is impossible. Foreign donors must construct a manageable list of critical incongruities of thought and practice between what they recommend and local practice (Department for International Development 2000; Stromsem 2000). Inclusive lists of all the political/social/legal factors that might be relevant are unhelpful. The first step is to describe in detail what successful implementation of democratic reform looks like, as illustrated in the algorithm of reform outlined in chapter 4. When this has been established, planners can ask country experts, as well as well as assistance practitioners who have had experience with similar programs elsewhere, whether adoption is possible in the particular circumstances and what local customs and practices might prevent it. Local recipients should be consulted in this process as well, for they are in the best position to say whether particular objectives are likely to be understood and accepted.

If democratic police reform is operationalized as adherence to the rule of law, observance of human rights, effective external accountability, and service responsiveness (chapter 2), what information do planners need about local circumstances in order to assist reform effectively? In other words, if not everything, then what? I suggest that the following information is crucial for developing plans for achieving respectively the four goals of democratic policing. This list is not exhaustive, but is a place to begin.

I. For the rule of law

1. The nature of political control over the police—whether it is close, mediated, or loose.
2. Whether political elites are involved with or beholding to criminal elements in society.
3. Whether the judiciary is independent from political control.
4. Whether access to government goods and services is based on clientage or impersonal rules.

II. For human rights

1. The legal status of human rights, especially association, speech, arrest/detention/exile, right to counsel, torture and use of force, self-incrimination, and privacy.
2. The commitment of police leaders to human rights and culture of human rights within the rank-and-file.
3. The public's respect for rights, especially the priority given to crime control over due process.

III. For accountability

1. Whether concepts crucial to our vision of democratic reform, such as "accountability," "responsiveness," and "community," are understood within local culture.
2. Whether there is separation of power in government between the executive and the judiciary.

3. How strong civil society, especially the press and non-governmental organizations, is in shaping public policy.
4. The openness of police and government to scrutiny from outside.
5. Where the power to control police is located politically—centrally, federally, or locally.

IV. For responsiveness

1. The operational policies of the police with respect to crime prevention, deployment, consultation with the public, and willingness to handle non-criminal requests for service.
2. The proportion of police work that is instigated by members of the public as opposed to government.
3. Whether access to the police has been made easy and convenient.
4. The customary demeanor of the police in contacts with the public—approachable, aloof, disdainful, forceful, and so on.
5. The degree of hostility toward police and its distribution socially and geographically.
6. Whether the management style of the police is directive, quasi-military, collegial, and so on.
7. The amount of initiative and responsibility allowed lower ranks within the police.
8. The education and competence of the police who are most in contact with citizens.
9. The extent and nature of police corruption.

Obviously, obtaining adequate information about matters even as select as these will be time consuming and will raise the cost of planning. In responding to unforeseen humanitarian emergencies, such an exercise may be impossible. Even in non-conflict environments, providers of developmental assistance will be tempted to skimp on this sort of preparation on the excuse that adjustments in implementation will always be necessary. One senior UN official has recommended deliberately keeping plans ambiguous, so that requirements developed far from the action do not hamper flexibility in the field (Covey 2003). This advice is too sweeping. Although all planning should be accepted as provisional until tested in the field, it is better to be forearmed against problems that experienced experts consider inevitable than to frustrate reform through lack of foresight. If problems can be avoided, they should be.

4. *Persuade Local Stakeholders to Support Reform*

Democratic reform requires the active support of the police at many levels and at least the acquiescence of politicians and the public. Obtaining "buy-in" is probably the most often cited lesson of security assistance (Blair and Lansen 1994; Carothers 1999b; Clegg, Hunt, and Whetton 2000; Commission on Post-Conflict Reconstruction 2003; Cordone 1999; Neild 2002; Oakley, Dziedzic, and Goldberg 1998; Popkin 1999). Foreign assistance, no matter how disinterested, substantial, or desirable, cannot create either an effective or a democratic police against the wishes of these crucial stakeholders.

Obtaining governmental buy-in despite entrenched interests is, therefore, the first obligation of a successful democratic reform program. Local political elites and police executives must understand the objectives of reform as clearly as donors. Without this "pull" from within, no amount of "push" from outside will produce reform. So important is this support for the success of foreign assistance that it should be considered a crucial element in judging whether foreign assistance should be undertaken at all.

All police reform is political in the sense that it affects the positions and interests of different groups of people both inside and outside the police (United Nations 2001). Resistance to reform is the rule rather than the exception. What foreigners regard as obstacles to reform, locals may find useful, such as corruptible police officers and politically subservient judges (Phillips, Fogelson, Ales, and Palmieri 2003). As a result, providers of assistance must accept the need to confront vested interests. Reform means upsetting applecarts; it is not politically antiseptic.

In order to obtain essential support for reform, assistance providers should formulate their plans in close consultation with local recipients. In this process they may locate and then support locals who have similar reform objectives. This requires a willingness on the part of providers to discuss reform plans with foreign governments before they are offered and to take the time to persuade stakeholders that proposed reforms are in their interest. This process works best when local governments have the capacity to formulate their own strategic plans, that is, to identify for themselves the specific inputs that are needed to achieve shared goals (Wedel 1998).

The best example of systematic collaboration in the design of police assistance for democratic reform is probably South Africa. Following the Mandela government's stated goal of "transforming" the police, the government discovered that by 1997 foreign assistance was being offered to the South African Police Service (SAPS) by over 200 separate entities—private, public, bi- and multilateral (Van der Spuy 1997). The programs were uncoordinated, each one justified in its own terms without reference to corporate plans of the South African police. In response, the government created the office of Donor Assistance Coordination within SAPS. It is responsible for ensuring that foreign assistance supports the strategic objectives of SAPS management, rather than the parochial objectives of separate units within it, and that the most critical needs as assessed by senior management are brought to the attention of international donors (Personal interview March 2000). In this way, the South African government controls the impact of foreign assistance and donors are reassured that their projects have top-level support. In 2003, the Donor Assistance office coordinated 50–60 projects, valued at approximately $50 million (Personal interview March 2003).

Similarly, the El Salvador government, following the peace accords of 1992, adopted an ambitious blueprint for police reform. Unfortunately, when crime rose dramatically in the late 1990s, the public became disillusioned with reform and pressed for a hard-line approach. Lou Cobarruviaz, ICITAP project director in El Salvador and former chief of police in San Jose, California, brought senior *Policía Nacional Civil* (PNC) executives to the United States to see for themselves the strategies being employed by progressive police departments. As a result, Cobarruviaz and the PNC developed PIP COM (Police Intervention/Community Policing Plan), involving intensive patrol, rapid response, and community consultation. With American support, the program was tried initially in two neighborhoods in San Salvador. PIP COM has been gradually expanded to others towns and regions.

Commitment to democratic police reform was entirely lacking on the part of local politicians in Bosnia-Herzegovina after the Dayton Accords, despite the lead given by the United Nations and

Dayton Accord donors. Reform was resisted at every step (Monk 2001). The respective governments in Bosnia-Herzegovina, especially in the Serb Republic, were unwilling to protect minorities, disband clandestine intelligence agencies, give up operational direction of the police, create a competent and independent judiciary, and raise police pay (Blair and Dziedzic 1997; International Crisis Group 2002; Perito 2004).

The critical importance of obtaining the support of local recipients creates a fundamental dilemma for the providers of police assistance. What is needed is often not what local officials want, yet the likelihood that assistance can make a significant difference depends almost entirely on whether they agree to support change. In effect, successful foreign assistance programs require both substantive good sense and procedural legitimacy. The problem is that in countries where substantive change is needed most, acceptance of change is likely to be most difficult to obtain. In order to obtain procedural legitimacy, donors may then be forced to reduce the scope of substantive change to what is locally acceptable.

This dilemma is especially acute for police reform in the context of peacekeeping. In peacekeeping, the United Nations or an ad hoc coalition of nations intervenes to create effective government in "failed" states. Outside leverage in these circumstances is maximal. The international community can do virtually what it wants in the short run with respect to civil administration. In the longer run, however, its ability to reconstruct local government according to its normative standards depends on making its imposition legitimate. Peacekeeping administrators must shift from "custodianship" through "partnership" to "ownership" (Hartz and Mercean 2003). In so doing, it becomes more and more necessary for peacekeepers to cede power over the content of reform. Gulliver must embrace the Tar Baby.

Democratic reform through foreign assistance must be seen as a process of negotiation, even though negotiation entails limiting the freedom of action of providers. As Richard Monk has observed, police reform is "as much about the issues of self-governance as about the transfer of policing skills"(2001).

This process of negotiation needs to involve the general public and not just political elites and the police (Klein 2001). There are several reasons for this.

First, the public may be as skeptical of the value of democratic policing as the police themselves, especially when crime is rising and public safety seems to be at risk. The public may condone torture, kill suspected criminals, and demand brutal punishments.

Second, a committed public can help to keep reform on track when elites and police lose enthusiasm and fall back into old habits.

Third, the development of greater responsiveness on the part of the police assumes that there is a public willing to be engaged. This is often not the case in countries where police have customarily been brutal and corrupt. People may need to be encouraged to give the police a chance to demonstrate that they have been reformed. Human-rights organizations and the media, whose stock-in-trade has been to publicize police misdeeds, must be willing to work collaboratively with the police in order to produce democratic reform (Neild 1999). Conducting this many-sided educational process is especially tricky for foreigners because it involves the creation of opinion within the country that constrains the actions of local government.

In sum, democratic reform may founder without buy-in from a range of stakeholders, including the general public. Obtaining this requires confronting the central problem of reform assistance: how to lead without causing resentment.

5. Treat Aid Recipients as Partners

Providers of assistance must guard against condescension in their relations with local police. The fact that a country needs foreign assistance does not mean that its people, including government officials, are unintelligent, backward, or incompetent.

Foreign providers are easy to resent. The very fact that they are in a country with advice, money, and leverage, conveys a message of superiority and, conversely, of local dependence. Americans, for example, may find that they are resented just because they are American. In Latin America, it is common for Hispanic-American advisors, even those whose mother tongue is Spanish, to be referred to as a *gringo*. In peacekeeping, the visible power and wealth of the international community is both dramatic and humbling. Military and civilian personnel commandeer buildings, inflate housing prices, and monopolize the best restaurants. Their distinctively marked vehicles seem to be everywhere. They live far beyond local standards and offer employment at exorbitant rates of pay.

There are several ways to reduce the imperial presumption of foreign assistance. First, local people should be treated as partners and consulted about the shape of reform. They should not, as Ignatieff says, "do the translating, cleaning and driving while the internationals do the grand imperial planning" (2002). Consultation is a technique for both obtaining buy-in and reducing the appearance of superiority. One device for doing this is to co-locate foreign project managers within the organization to be reformed, thus enforcing more collaborative relationships. The European Union has been doing this with the police in South Africa and Bosnia-Herzegovina.

Second, providers of foreign assistance should train and appoint local people as program managers. Locals, provided they are competent and committed, will be more effective as "change agents" than foreigners because they have local standing and local knowledge (Carothers 1999b). They may also be more sensitive to cultural problems of transferability. For the same reasons, experts from other countries who have dealt with similar conditions can also be useful as project managers.

Third, foreign reformers must be trained to recognize the competence, skill, and intelligence of the people they advise. Senior police officers in Bosnia-Herzegovina, most of whom were college graduates, resented being tutored by advisors from third-world countries whose professionalism was considerably less than their own (Monk, Holm, and Rumin 2001). As one university-educated senior officer said, "What the hell do I have to learn from a 25-year-old Ghanaian sergeant?" Similarly, advisors from the first world must be careful not to discount out of hand the skills of police in "less advanced" countries. Local officers may be more effective at solving crime in local settings than better-educated and more technologically experienced foreign advisors, even within democratic rules. In short, effective advising requires a sensitive appreciation of the value of local practice. As a rule, advisors should concentrate on demonstrating the value of the new rather than condemning the old.

Fourth, foreign reformers should connect local police with professional networks of progressive police internationally, such as the International Association of Chiefs of Police, the International Police Association, the International Association of Civilian Oversight of

Law Enforcement, and the International Association of Police Trainers. International exchanges of personnel can also be useful, as when police stations are "twinned" with others abroad or police from pilot projects are sent to observe similar operations elsewhere.

6. *Coordinate Assistance Efforts*

In order to be administered effectively, foreign assistance for democratic development must be coordinated among donors in the field as well as among agencies within donor governments. The number of donors is often so great that one needs a scorecard to keep track—UN peacekeeping missions; separate UN agencies, such as the United Nations High Commissioner for Refugees, the United Nations Human Rights Commission, and the United Nations Development Programme; regional governmental organizations, such as the European Union, the Council of Europe, and the Organization for Security and Co-operation in Europe; a host of country-donors, most from the first world (United States, Canada, Great Britain, France, Germany, Denmark, Netherlands, Sweden, Norway, Australia, Japan); several quasi-government organizations, such as the British Council and the U.S. Institute for Peace; and a few private foundations, such as Soros, Ford, and Wallenberg. Each of these may have different goals, adopt distinctive strategies, insist on unique administrative requirements for receiving aid, and bombard hard-pressed officials with requests for access and support (Rule of Law Working Group 1994, Stromsem 2000, Van der Spuy 1999, United Nations Development Programme 2001).

Lack of coherence in training is one of the most common problems of coordination, involving differences in marching and drill, crime scene protection, evidence collection, vehicle chases, firearms technique, shooting objectives, and use of handcuffs. Because there is no agreement internationally about police doctrine, advisors teach what they know at home, leading to what one official referred to as "foreign feudalism" as each country imposes its own procedures in whatever area of training it has been given. In Bosnia-Herzegovina, for example, crowd control has been taught by the United States, France, and Germany; interviewing techniques by Great Britain, Denmark, the United Nations High Commissioner for Refugees, and the U.S. Immigration and Naturalization Services (International Crisis Group 2002). A Bosnian officer reported that UN personnel from India, Uganda, Somalia, and Denmark had significantly different conceptions of community policing. At the new police academy in El Salvador in 1995, instruction was offered by 40 foreign advisors from five countries (United States, Spain, Chile, Norway, and Sweden) (Costa 1995).

One solution would be for donors to coordinate their programs with respect to purpose, strategy, doctrine, and implementation, so as to avoid duplication, make use of the comparative advantage of different donors, and simplify administrative requirements for recipients (Commission on Post-Conflict Reconstruction 2003; Department for International Development 2002; Diamond 1995; Neild 2002). Yet this is unlikely to happen for several reasons. Because policing touches so intimately the nature of government, doctrinal differences reflect hallowed patterns of political and legal accommodation worked out at home. They are difficult to rethink, let alone to set aside in favor of different but normatively congruent practices. Furthermore, there is "ferocious competition" for foreign markets for security products, leverage over local governments, and achievement of donors' foreign policy goals (Ignatieff 2002). Finally, local recipients often prefer competition among donors because it increases their freedom of action. Local officials play one provider off another, thereby retaining more control.

Another solution to the diversity of assistance inputs is for the receiving governments themselves to impose coordination on donors. This is what South Africa has done. The Office of Donor Assistance Coordination of the South African Police Service holds quarterly meetings with donors to share information about what South African needs and to coordinate inputs. The problem with this solution is that countries that are the targets of the most diverse assistance are exactly the countries that are least able to coordinate it on their own. The South African model may be difficult to replicate in the places that need it most.

A variation on this solution is for receiving countries to allow the monopolization of police assistance by a single foreign donor. Local officials see this as a great simplification, provided, of course, that they have a "special relationship" with the dominant provider that ensures sufficient assistance to sustain police development and reform. El Salvador has done this with respect to the United States (Rosa de Leon-Escribano 2000).

But coordination among international donors is only part of the problem. Donors themselves, especially governments, may offer fragmented, contradictory, and duplicative programs. This happens because different agencies of the same government use foreign assistance for different purposes. The great divide in police assistance is between programs designed to enhance law-enforcement capacity and programs designed to develop democratic practices. As a partial remedy for this, the United States recently created the post of "Security Coordinator" in several of its embassies, primarily in Latin America and the states of the former Soviet Union. This person is responsible for coordinating requests for assistance based on shared analysis of local needs among its several security agencies (FBI, DEA, Customs, Secret Service, Immigration and Naturalization Service, and Diplomatic Security). Similarly, the United Nations has begun to bring people together from its military and police commands within the Department of Peacekeeping Operations, the UN Development Programme, and the High Commissioner for Human Rights to formulate post-conflict civil reconstruction plans.

There is a final dimension to the problem of coordinating police assistance programs abroad, namely, the relationship between assistance personnel in the field and policy managers at home. Field personnel often complain that the home office doesn't understand local conditions, micromanages their activities, and requires formulaic, unhelpful, and time-consuming reporting. Home offices, on the other hand, complain that field personnel don't see the "big picture," change programs without consultation, and are too deferential to local stakeholders. Although managing this relationship would seem to be a relatively small problem, it is a constant source of tension in the working lives of assistance personnel. Research has shown that most of the stress felt by people in service professions comes from their relations with colleagues—peers and superiors—rather than their relations with clients (Cherniss 1980; Toch 2002). Anecdotal evidence suggests that this is very much the case in the administration of foreign assistance.

7. Send the Right People into the Field

In order to do the planning, persuading, partnering, and coordinating that is essential for the successful administration of development assistance to the police, the right people must be recruited, trained, and sent into the field.

First, the design and implementation of democratic police development should be done largely by personnel with experience in what is called full-service policing. It requires advisors who know first-hand what it is like to accommodate simultaneously the stipulations of law, the directives of elected politicians, and the needs of a diverse public. In particular, if responsiveness to the needs of individuals is accepted as one of the hallmarks of democratic policing, then advisors need to come from agencies that understand what it is like to be accountable to the public individually as well as to governments collectively. This is a particular problem for the United States. Although most policing in the United States is done by state and local agencies, foreign assistance is provided by the national government whose law enforcement personnel specialize, for the most part, in criminal investigation and proactive crime prevention (FBI, DEA, Marshall Service, INS, Secret Service). In order for the U.S. government to provide professional advice and training in democratic policing as opposed to law-enforcement capacity-building, it must involve state and local law-enforcement personnel. Doing so, however, is costly, more so than detaching federal personnel for limited periods. Furthermore, state and local agencies accustomed to pleading for money to hire additional personnel are understandably reluctant to part with experienced officers.

Second, providing police assistance in support of democratic development is too complicated to be left to police alone. It needs the skills and insight of civilians experienced in public-sector management, foreign area studies, law, oversight and accountability processes, crime prevention, and the dynamics of criminal justice systems (Barkan 1997; Boisevert, Menard, and Ostiguy 2000)

Third, selection of personnel for foreign assistance missions needs to be guided by an assessment of the tasks to be carried out. Generalists, whether police or civilian, are unlikely to have the skills needed to successfully implement all the activities called for in democratic police reform. This is especially true when a foreign police is being wholly reconstructed, as in peacekeeping (Brahimi Report 2000; Dwan 2002; International Association of Peacekeeping Training Centres 1999; Monk 2001). UNCIVPOL has been called upon to monitor, advise, train, equip, certify, patrol, investigate, and arrest all at the same time. Obviously, this requires a team of people with diverse skills.

It also follows that people should not be recruited, no matter how skilled, who do not bring professional commitment to the job. Overseas assignment is more than a retirement benefit or a chance to travel at someone else's expense (McHugh 1994).

Fourth, the people who implement police assistance must understand what democracy means in terms of police practice. Recruiting people from non-democratic countries to develop democratic policing, as the United Nations does, is not a good idea (Neild 1995; Perito 2004; Swedish National Police Board 2000). Unfortunately, recruiting people from democratic countries is not a guaranteed solution either. A survey of UNCIVPOL personnel in Bosnia in 1996 found that knowledge of human rights did not vary by nationality (Marotta 1999). Very often advisors from developed democracies assume that whatever is done at home is conformable with democracy. This is a dangerous conceit not only because countries with praiseworthy democratic records may have become accustomed to practices that violate their own standards, but also because practices that are benign in one context can undermine democratic development in another. Since different institutional devices may be used to achieve similar goals, advisors need to be able to analyze the potentiality for democratic reform in the customary practices of a local setting. This kind of diagnosis requires unusual talent and insight, more than can be expected of typical aid personnel or volunteer police officers. It follows, therefore, that democratic police assistance must be provided by carefully constructed teams of experts who act in concert, with regular opportunities to discuss problems and formulate solutions.

Fifth, people selected to implement democratic reform and reconstruction abroad, especially those with operational backgrounds, should receive specialized training in managing the process of change abroad. Obviously the content of training, as well as its length, will vary with job assignments. For example, senior managers need broader training than firearms instructors (Perito 2004; Schoenhaus 2002; Sweden 2002). Such training should minimally specify the content of democratic policing, explore the variety of mechanisms that have been used to institutionalize it, and provide practical examples from international experience of the difficulties of fitting foreign practices to local conditions.

Sixth, foreigners assigned to produce change abroad must reside in-country for substantial periods of time. This is necessary in order to provide programmatic continuity, informed advice, and expeditious midcourse corrections (Carothers 1999; Democratization Policy Institute 2002; Sweden 2002; Wedel 1998). Although observers differ about the optimal length of time for deployment, they all agree that for advisory personnel it should be measured in years not months. The Brahimi panel report (2000) criticized UNCIVPOL's customary deployments of six months as being too short. As a cantonal Minister in Bosnia said, after dealing successively with an American, an Austrian, and a Russian advisor from the United Nations International Police Task Force, "I'm tired of explaining" (Personal interview 2002).

On the other hand, advisors can also stay too long. They may become too comfortable in jobs that involve little immediate responsibility, where hours of work are discretionary, remuneration is exceptional, and the status gained considerable.

Seventh, the behavior of people who provide assistance abroad must be monitored closely, and misbehaving officers should be immediately relieved of duty and sent home. This is particularly important for uniformed police personnel deployed alongside local operational personnel. The ability of assistance providers to persuade others to adopt new procedures and behave in new ways depends in large part on the example they set. To gain legitimacy, they must accept responsibility for being a role model.

Conclusion

In order to institutionalize democratic police practices abroad, the providers of foreign assistance must plan, commit, adapt, persuade, partner, coordinate, and staff. The implementation of democratic assistance is not simple. It takes unusual skill and must be thoughtfully done.

Fortunately, the ability of the international community to manage democratic assistance programs may be growing. It is not generally recognized that during the last fifteen years an international cadre of reform specialists has been created that has had extensive hands-on experience in justice sector reform, including the police. A few of these have been employed by NGOs, but most have been government employees, both national and international. Some have done explicit reconstruction work, as with the United Nations in Bosnia, Kosovo, or East Timor. Others have been involved in building law-enforcement capacity under bilateral auspices. This is true, for example, of many American FBI and DEA agents.

Some of the people assigned or recruited to work abroad have discovered that they like the work and want to make a career of it. They find the life of a police advisor abroad attractive for several reasons.

First, the work they do is often a lot more challenging than what they were doing before. Instead of doing repetitious operational tasks, like directing traffic or responding to calls for service, they are planning, managing, and monitoring the activities of police stations or, indeed, of entire police forces. In effect, foreign assignment is a functional promotion.

Second, they have a heady sense of being involving in consequential activities, of being part of history in a way they never will be at home, and of making a dramatic difference in the lives of people who are desperate and traumatized.

Third, working abroad is an adventure—meeting new people, speaking new languages, seeing new sights, and sometimes living dangerously.

Fourth, assignment abroad develops an intense sense of camaraderie among participants, very much as military service does. Assistance personnel, particularly in peacekeeping missions, feel like pioneers who share "the mystique of selfless commitment, reinforced by an oral tradition of hardship, ingenuity, determination, and ultimate success" (Schoenhaus 2002).

Fifth, despite the hardships of "deployment shock," most international assistance personnel live comfortably and exercise considerable authority. They are paid well not only by local standards but also in comparison to salaries and perks at home. This is especially true if foreign assignment is a second career. Furthermore, as part of peacekeeping missions they enjoy enormous status, somewhat like being colonial administrators (Ignatieff 2002). They are a visible part of the biggest show in town.

For all these reasons, people who have served in foreign assistance missions often speak about the difficulty of "coming down" after returning home. Foreign assignment is a "high" that can't be shared with people who haven't been there.

In addition to providing a reservoir of talent, the development of this new international occupation may have another potentially important benefit: it may encourage police reform in the countries that provide assistance as well as in those that receive it. Serving together abroad, members of international missions learn from one another. In fact, some countries require their nationals to write assessment reports about their experience; a few systematically debrief returnees. In this way, good ideas are discovered and shared. Furthermore, participants have had a unique opportunity to compare what is being done abroad with customary practice at home. They have been put in situations where they have been forced to consider whether policing can be done differently. As a result, whether they recognize it or not, they have become potential change-agents at home. In the long run, this cadre of experienced assistance specialists may contribute to the formulation of de facto standards of democratic policing, exemplified increasingly within countries on both the giving and the receiving end of assistance.

7

Evaluating Impact

The United States and the larger international community have used foreign assistance to promote police reform as part of encouraging the development of democratic government. Considerable investment both human and material has been made in this strategy. Does it work? Has international assistance made foreign police significantly more democratic and thus contributed to the establishment of democratic government? This chapter will attempt to answer this question. It will focus primarily on the impact of American assistance, with some commentary on multinational experience.

As a general proposition, American foreign assistance has not been shown to contribute significantly or consistently to reforming police institutions abroad, still less to the creation and stabilization of democratic governments. The reasons for saying this are discussed in section one of this chapter. Because available evidence suggests that democratic police reform is an uncertain business, with many factors stacked against it, it is reasonable to ask whether police reform programs should be undertaken at all, but, if so, where and when. This will be discussed in the second section. Finally, assessing the impact of foreign assistance is a difficult business. Evaluation is essential, however, in order to develop sound assistance policy and to implement it successfully in the field. The third section will examine the problems of evaluating the impact of democratic police assistance abroad and will offer suggestions for making evaluation more meaningful and practical.

Evidence of Impact

American assistance to police abroad is viewed as a means for achieving three goals—creation of democratic governments, institutionalization of democratic police practices, and improvement in law-enforcement capacity. Evidence for the impact of foreign assistance on each of these will be examined.

Assistance and Democratic Government

During the latter part of the 20th century, the number of countries with democratic governments increased substantially. According to one major inventory, between 1978 and 1994 the ratio of democracies to autocracies reversed, from two to one against democracy to two to one in favor (Gurr, Marshall, and Khosla 2001). Since 1989 particularly, the number of democracies has increased, as has the number of transitional regimes. Although this trend cannot be attributed to reform assistance, it suggests that reform assistance has been working with the grain of global development.

American military interventions abroad and subsequent political development efforts, sometimes undertaken in concert with others, have not been notably successful in creating democratic governments (Zeller 2003). Of 13 cases since 1900, only four countries became democracies—Germany and Japan after World War II, which were examples of multilateral intervention, and Grenada (1983) and Panama (1989), exclusively American operations. Democracy did not develop after military interventions in Cambodia (1970–1973), Cuba (1906–1909 and 1917–1922), Dominican Republic (1965–1966), Haiti (1915–1934 and 1994–1996), Nicaragua (1909–1927), and South Vietnam (1964–1973).

The U.S. government's General Accounting Office (GAO) conducted an analysis of the impact of democracy assistance on countries in Latin America and the Caribbean, specifically programs to develop the rule of law, administrative transparency and accountability, respect for human rights, and free and fair elections (U.S. General Accounting Office 2003). From 1992 to 2002 the U.S. government invested slightly more than one billion dollars in such programs in the region, half of it ($580 million) going to six countries—Bolivia, Colombia, El Salvador, Guatemala, Nicaragua, and Peru. Using the scoring by Freedom House measuring changes made in political rights and civil liberties in those countries, the GAO concluded that democracy programs had "a modest impact." As table 7.1 shows, political rights and civil liberties improved in four of the six countries, remained the same in one, and got worse in another. The GAO reported some success in enacting new criminal procedure codes, improving the capacity in municipalities to manage budgets, increasing attention to human rights, and holding elections judged to be free and fair. But progress was spotty. Some countries didn't enact new criminal codes and, when they did, failed to implement them; local governments generally did not take effective action against corruption; and programs to improve justice training and equipment languished when aid stopped.

The General Accounting Office also evaluated the impact of rule-of-law programs in countries of the former Soviet Union in the first decade after independence (1992–2002) (U.S. General Account-

Table 7.1
Democracy and U.S. Assistance in Latin America

Countries	Democracy Assistance (in U.S. millions)	1992 Score	2002 Score	Change
Bolivia	63.3	2.5	2.0	Better
Peru	64.6	4.0	2.0	Better
Guatemala	69.5	4.0	3.5	Better
Nicaragua	88.3	3.0	3.0	Same
El Salvador	145.8	3.5	2.5	Better
Colombia	149.1	3.0	4.0	Worse

Note: Scores range from 1 (most free) to 7 (least free).

ing Office 2001). American investment of over $200 million, the GAO concluded, had "limited impact," with the countries of the new independent states scoring "poorly in the development of the rule of law and, as a whole, . . . growing worse over time." In fact, in Russia and Ukraine, the two biggest recipients of rule-of-law assistance, the situation deteriorated. Only in Georgia, Moldova, and Tajikistan was there improvement.

Reviewing American assistance efforts since the mid-1980s, Thomas Carothers reports a similarly mixed picture for American democracy and rule-of-law assistance (1999). He believes it helped to sustain transitions to democracy in Guatamala and Romania, but did not help in Nepal and Zambia. "What stands out," says another observer, "about rule-of-law assistance . . . is how difficult and often disappointing such work is" (Golub 2003).

Altogether, democracy building abroad is a chancy enterprise, depending more on local conditions than foreign initiative, even when those initiatives are undertaken with overwhelming authority as in the case of military intervention.

Assistance and Democratic Policing

If the record of foreign assistance is equivocal with respect to the development of democratic government in general, what about its effects on the practices of policing? Have police become more democratic as a result of American assistance efforts? Unfortunately it is impossible to answer this question in any systematic way because comparative information about local police institutions is lacking. International data sets constructed to enable comparison among countries contain hardly any items pertaining to the character of police practices. Moreover, it is very difficult to determine the amount and nature of American police assistance to different countries so that impact can be reliably compared. All the problems of estimating assistance to the police described in chapter 3 occur again for each country. Country analyses are essential, however, because it is only through case studies using longitudinal analysis that connections can be demonstrated between assistance inputs and reform outputs.

Judgments about the success that development assistance, American and otherwise, has had in reforming police abroad are, at the moment, almost entirely qualitative. That is, they are based on the impressions of field personnel or informed observers such as scholars and consultants (Call 1999a; Call and Stanley 1999; Hansen 2002; Huggins 1998; Cottam and Marenin 1989). During the 1990s, concerted efforts at police reform were made in many places—Angola, El Salvador, Guatemala, Bosnia-Herzegovina, Liberia, Northern Ireland, Kosovo, East Timor, Namibia, Poland, East Germany, the Czech Republic, Occupied Territories of Palestine, Hungary, Romania, Haiti, Eastern Slavonia, Rwanda, Somalia, South Africa, Haiti, Cambodia, Sierra Leone, Nicaragua, Mozambique, Ukraine, Poland, and Western Sahara. Summarizing many qualitative judgments, the results are mixed. Reform was judged not to have been sustained in Angola, Bosnia-Herzegovina, Colombia, Haiti, Liberia, Rwanda, Somalia, Ukraine, and Western Sahara. On the other hand, significant and sustainable reform was achieved in Northern Ireland, Eastern Slavonia, Mozambique, El Salvador, South Africa, Namibia, and East Germany. Generalizing about features that determine success will be difficult from these gleanings because the level and character of reform assistance from the international community varied enormously among the countries where success was thought to have been achieved.

The largest American effort at police reform since 1990 took place in Latin America, Eastern and Central Europe, and the former Soviet Union. Qualitative results, again, are mixed. In Latin America, El Salvador is considered to be an outstanding success (Call 1999b; interviews in El Salvador 2002; Neild 2002; U.S. General Accounting Office 2003). Following the 1991 Peace Accords, the United States provided crucial help, largely through the International Criminal Investigation Training Assistance Program (ICI-TAP), in redrafting basic laws, restructuring the police, developing a strategic crime prevention program, improving the managerial capabilities of the police, creating a new police academy, and connecting the police more responsively to the public. Such reforms were an important component of El Salvador's successful transition to democracy (Gurr, Marshall, and Khosla 2001). Haiti, on the other hand, was an outstanding failure (Beidas, Granderson, and Neild 2003; Stromsem and Trincellito 2003). According to the GAO, the U.S. government spent about $70 million on programs of assistance to the Haitian police between 1994 and 1999. The work was carried out by ICITAP, the Department of the Treasury, the Coast Guard, the U.S. Customs Service, and the Drug Enforcement Administration. Despite this effort, the GAO concluded, the "[Haitian] police force has not effectively carried out its basic law enforcement responsibilities, and . . . politicization has compromised the force" (U.S. General Accounting Office 2002). This judgment was made before American intervention in March 2004, following the collapse of the Aristide government.

In eastern and central Europe and the former Soviet Union, observers see a great change in the rhetoric of policing but little in its practice. Although police officials and politicians in those countries routinely describe what they are doing in terms of democracy, accountability, transparency, and community policing, behavior continues to reflect the authoritarian habits of the recent past (Caparini and Marenin 2003).

In Bosnia-Herzegovina, the international community intervened massively and authoritatively after the Dayton Accords (December 1995) to reshape police institutions. The United States made a major contribution to this effort bilaterally through ICITAP and multilaterally through its support of UNCIVPOL. Beginning in 1996, the United Nations Mission in Bosnia-Herzegovina purged the police of people who had committed human rights abuses, substantially reduced the number of police, created a State Border Service, set up new police academies in Sarajevo and Banja Luka, improved greater cooperation between the police of the Croat-Muslim Federation and the Serb Republic, and completed the certification of all Federation police officers (Hansen 2002; United Nations 2002a; United Nations Mission in Bosnia and Herzegovina 2002). Through ICITAP, the American government developed detailed policy and procedure manuals for the police, held management seminars for senior- and middle-ranking officers, helped to develop curricula for the new police academies, provided resident advisors to senior policy makers, and introduced community policing (U.S. Department of Justice, Criminal Division 2002).

Despite the tangible accomplishments of the longest lasting police-assistance effort of modern times, most observers consider reform in Bosnia-Herzegovina to be superficial and are pessimistic about its sustainability once international monitoring is withdrawn (Hansen 2002). The International Crisis Group described the rule of law in BiH as a "disaster." And a report from the United Nations

Development Programme said there had been "tremendous effort with minimal results" (United Nations Development Programme 2001). According to recent assessments, the administration of justice remains under the control of politicians, corruption is rampant, organized crime works hand-in-glove with local governments, law is enforced unequally among ethnic groups, minimal efforts have been made to recruit minorities, and intelligence gathering is shaped by political agendas (International Crisis Group 2002; Monk 2001; United Nations 2002).

These doubts about the depth and sustainability of justice reform in Bosnia-Herzegovina should not obscure the larger humanitarian achievements of international intervention. The most deadly conflict in Europe since World War II was stopped, refugees have returned in substantial numbers, ethnic armies have been demobilized, elections have been held, basic laws revised, and human rights violations detected and perpetrators punished. The long-term prospects for democracy may be questionable, but governance throughout the Croat-Muslim Federation and the Serb Republic, while not exemplary, is a huge improvement over what it was, a fact generally appreciated by their war-weary publics.

Against these equivocal examples of reform assistance, South Africa is generally considered a heartening success. Following the 1994 elections, the first truly free and representative elections in South African history, the Mandela government initiated not just reform but what it described as a "transformation" of the police. The transformation involved increasing the representation of blacks at senior ranks, developing a national crime-prevention strategy, introducing community policing, emphasizing responsive service delivery, reforming public order policing, promoting affirmative action for women and minorities, and strengthening internal discipline and accountability (Bruce 2003b; Guru, Marshall, and Khosla 2001; Marks 2002; South African Police Service, n.d.; van der Spuy 1997, 1999). Many of these elements speak directly to the four criteria for democratic policing outlined in chapter 2. In addition, the South African Police Service developed its own mechanism for coordinating international police assistance to ensure that it fit South African objectives.

In sum, evaluations of the impact of foreign assistance on police reform, almost all of which rely on qualitative observations, show that assistance to the police can have a positive effect in some cases, but that success is by no means the rule.

Assistance and Law-Enforcement Effectiveness

One might think that it is easier to evaluate the success of assistance given to improve law-enforcement effectiveness than for democratic reform because the objective is more concrete, perhaps more susceptible to quantitative measure. This is not the case. Criminologists dispute endlessly about how much, if any, the police and other institutions of criminal justice contribute to public safety (Bayley 1994; Eck and Maguire 2000; Levitt 1994; Nagin 1998; Skogan and Frydl 2003; Walker 1989). As the South African Police Service sensibly observed, "[T]he starting point to bear in mind is that the effectiveness of police work within a society is nearly impossible to measure" (South African Police Service n.d.). The problem is compounded in the very countries that have attracted most assistance because of their inability to collect reliable information about crime and disorder. The upshot is that there are few careful, systematic, objective evaluations of the impact of foreign assistance on police capabilities abroad. Even more than is the case with democratic assistance, evaluation consists largely of inventories of programs delivered, equipment installed, and money spent. Presumably the experts providing such aid have formed judgments about whether the assistance has made a difference, but these opinions rarely become a matter of public record.

With respect to American assistance, the GAO has once again done the only general evaluation of this dimension of police assistance. Examining law-enforcement training within rule-of-law programs in countries of the former Soviet Union between 1992 and 2000, the GAO found that few of the techniques taught were being "routinely applied" (U.S. General Accounting Office 2001), and doubted that criminal-investigation training had much impact on local capabilities. This finding was sharply disputed by the Department of Justice, whose agencies were largely responsible for its administration, specifically, the FBI, the DEA, the International Law Enforcement Academy in Budapest, and the FBI and DEA academies at Quantico, Virginia. In response, the GAO said that because it could find only two relevant evaluations, it would withhold judgment one way or the other. In effect, it was saying that if there was evidence of positive effect, let the implementing agencies produce it.

Examining ICITAP's efforts to develop the investigation capabilities of police in six Latin American countries, the GAO concluded that they had "limited" impact (U.S. General Accounting Office 2003). This echoes the general assessment of Hilderbrand and Grindle that American capacity-building initiatives in the 1990s "have not paid off in terms of improved effectiveness or higher levels of organizational or individual performance" (1997).

At the beginning of the chapter I asked whether foreign assistance to the police contributed as hoped to democratic development. Did it make the police more democratic and thus support transitions to democratic government? Based on available evaluations, I conclude:

1. It is unrealistic to expect that providing assistance to the police will achieve democratic government, although it may be a component in that endeavor.
2. Assistance can prompt reform in police practices but it may be superficial and short-lived.
3. The impact of assistance on local law-enforcement capabilities is unknown.

In sum, based on the available evidence, the impact of foreign assistance on either democratic government or police practice appears to be slight.

There is an additional and important conclusion that can be drawn. When foreign assistance has led to significant change, it seems to have confirmed initiatives already planned or started by foreign governments rather than moving police in new directions. This mirrors experience with government grants for police innovation in the United States. The U.S. government spent over $8 billion between 1995 and 2000 under the Safe Streets Act (1994) to support community policing, a sum far exceeding what it has spent abroad on foreign police assistance. An exhaustive study by the Kennedy School of Government, Harvard University, found that federal assistance reinforced local decisions about what to do, but did not change them (Moore et al. 1999). Abroad and at home, then, assistance is a weak lever for producing significant change if governments are not already persuaded that the planned reforms are desirable. This reinforces a point about reform tactics made in chapter 6: obtaining the commitment ("buy-in") of local recipients to reform goals is absolutely essential to success.

The Calculus of Democratic Assistance

Given what is known about the effects of foreign assistance on democracy and particularly its police institutions, should the United States and others continue to invest in this strategy? The lack of connection between police assistance and the creation of democratic governments should not be surprising. Few people would argue that the police tail can wag the political dog. The more interesting question is whether foreign assistance can facilitate the reform of police institutions themselves. Experience indicates that there are two sets of impediments—problems with programs and problems with countries.

With respect to program problems, I have already discussed issues of strategy and tactics (chapters 4 and 6), including the tension between security and reform (chapter 5). But three larger problems need to be borne in mind as well.

First: Assistance is given to foreign police for many reasons, not all of them connected to the goal of democratic reform—to enhance law-enforcement capability, increase or maintain influence, obtain support on particular international issues, develop markets, stop conflict, alleviate humanitarian emergencies, and obtain cooperation in fighting criminal threats from abroad. Although by law American assistance programs are never to be undertaken at the expense of human rights, democratic reform is rarely their primary objective.

Second: The amount of police assistance given is small in relation to the size of the enterprise that it is intended to affect. The GAO estimated, for example, that the United States spent $216 million over eight years on rule-of-law programs in the former Soviet Union. That amounts to $27 million per year dispersed among 14 countries, some of which, like Russia and Ukraine, have enormous population by world standards (150 million and 52 million respectively). Although the GAO carefully observes that funding levels were not "necessarily a significant factor limiting impact and sustainability," it would be naive not to discount the likely effectiveness of assistance by the size of the country to be affected (U.S. General Accounting Office 2001).

Third: Political and bureaucratic reform cannot be accomplished in a short period of time. Most of the assistance programs that have been evaluated have run for a few years—ten in the case of Latin America and eight in the former Soviet Union (U.S. General Accounting Office 2001, 2003). It is unreasonable to expect investments of these magnitudes to have achieved their objectives so soon.

In addition to the problems of mixed purposes, inadequate scale, and short timeframes, the success of reform assistance depends upon conditions within recipient countries. People involved in police assistance programs cite a daunting list of circumstances that have hampered success: lack of local commitment, rising crime and violence, corruption, antiquated infrastructures, dysfunctional administrative systems, authoritarian managerial styles, uneducated rank-and-file, politically subservient judiciaries, bureaucratic rivalry between the police and other sectors of the criminal justice system, and distrustful, hostile publics.

Because conditions like these are encountered in almost any country where democratic police reform would be undertaken, should one conclude that almost any program of foreign assistance for police reform is doomed to failure? There are certainly circumstances so unfavorable to democratic reform that the costs of involvement far outweigh any likely benefits. In fact, the United State has occasionally terminated police assistance programs for precisely this reason. It did so in Haiti in 2000 and Liberia in 1997. At the same time, because there have been occasional successes, it would be premature to conclude that foreign assistance can never facilitate democratic police reform abroad. What we need is a select list of conditions that indicates when reform assistance can make a constructive difference and, minimally, when reform assistance is certain to fail. In other words, analysis needs to be undertaken about the facilitators, on one hand, and prerequisites, on the other, for successful reform assistance.

As a beginning to this exercise, I suggest there are two sets of conditions that make reform highly unlikely, one applying to the political context within which reform is to take place and the other to the police themselves (Costa 1995; Stanley 1996a; U.S. Agency for International Development 1998; Washington Office on Latin America 1995; Washington Office on Latin America and the American University School of International Service 1990). In effect, these are my no-go conditions.

A. Political context

1. Conflict that makes effective government impossible.
2. Suppression of human rights as a matter of government policy rather than institutional failure.
3. Lack of commitment by political leaders to the principles of democratic reform.
4. Absence of civilian control of the police.
5. Unwillingness to provide essential material support to sustaining police reform.
6. Record of non-compliance with previous foreign assistance requirements.

B. Police institutions

1. Leadership uncommitted to the four elements of democratic reform.
2. Continuing and knowing violation of human rights.
3. Unwillingness to recruit and promote on merit.
4. Unwillingness to revise and restructure training.

Although experts on foreign assistance disagree about whether assistance for police reform should be withheld or terminated under circumstances such as these, they accept that grading countries with respect to the likely impact of assistance is feasible and appropriate. Such analysis often leads to a tripartite grouping of countries. First, foreign assistance might achieve "surprising successes" at democracy building in countries that are peaceful and democratically disposed already (Gurr, Marshall, and Khosla 2001, Carothers 1999a, U.S. Agency for International Development 1994). Second, assistance might (although not for certain) reinforce democratic initiatives in countries that are seriously trying to transform repressive into democratic governments (Gurr, Marshall, and Khosla 2001, Carothers 1999a). Third, assistance is unlikely to have any positive effect in confirmed autocracies or countries retreating from democratic reforms (Gurr, Marshall, and Khosla 2001). Triage is the treatment model that is implied by this clustering, where foreign assistance is concentrated on the second category, withheld from the third, and provided more symbolically than instrumentally to the first. Thomas Carothers has argued that democracy assistance might serve a useful function even in the third group by providing "voice" for a democratic alternative—not by investing in operational reform but by spreading knowledge of democratic alternatives (1999a). Furthermore, as USAID has pointed out, the United States might have other interests altogether in repressive, autocratic states, such as the maintenance of alliances or developing cooperation against international crime, that would justify foreign assistance (U.S. Agency for International Development 1994).

Looked at strictly from the point of view of achieving democratic reform of police, triage seems to me to be the appropriate paradigm. Assistance should be concentrated in the first two categories, provided the prerequisite conditions continue to exist, but should not be given where there is unyielding obstruction and fundamental principles are compromised.

Improving Evaluation

Although the importance of evaluation is acknowledged throughout the assistance agencies of the U.S. government, rigorous, systematic evaluation of American reform programs abroad is lacking at the present time. By and large, evaluations are superficial, a mechanical collection of information largely about what agencies are doing or hope to do rather than what they accomplish (Carothers 1999a). In the words of the GAO, evaluations of democracy assistance do not provide useful "knowledge about the impact and sustainability of projects in different countries" (U.S. General Accounting Office 2001, 2003). Assessments of police assistance programs are hampered by the absence of critical information, in particular total budgetary outlays for such programs across the U.S. government and inventories of police-related programs by country (United Nations Development Programme 2001). In other words, it is difficult to determine exactly what the U.S. government is doing and where.

There is also a fundamental intellectual problem. There is no agreement on the standard for determining success. Evaluations variously invoke changes in the quality of political life, specific changes in police organization or policy, impressions of whether police performance is better or worse than the past, the likelihood that improvements will be sustained, and simply whether programs were implemented as intended. Evaluations rarely measure success in terms of changes in international rankings along similar dimensions, such as free elections or the rule of law, the sort of information provided by the United Nations report on global democratization and by Freedom House. Nor do they stipulate criteria in terms of their own goals and construct measures for them. Finally, perceptions of success also reflect assessments, largely subjective, about the importance of assistance in affecting perceived changes. Was it crucial, helpful, or irrelevant?

It will be difficult to relate expenditures to results only because there are no databases aggregating information about police institutions and practices in countries internationally. Moreover, what little information there is about the performance of police with respect to crime control and the maintenance of public order—their core purpose—is very unreliable. It follows, therefore, that if donors are serious about evaluation, reform-assistance programs should include funds to enable recipient agencies abroad to improve the collection of information about their own activities. This should also contribute critically to the development of evidence-based policing, which, as I argued in chapter 5, is a key element in effective crime control. A requirement that reform assistance contain money for evaluation would benefit both policy making at home and the development of police professionalism abroad.

If evaluation of the impact of justice assistance is to be undertaken successfully, several procedural points need to be borne in mind.

First: It is widely assumed that the key to evaluation is the choice of performance indicators. This is not the case because it puts the cart before the horse. The first step in evaluation is to specify what the programs to be evaluated are supposed to achieve (VERA Institute of Justice 2003). Policy makers who turn evaluation over to evaluation consultants without stipulating program goals lose control over the terms by which they will be judged. On the other hand, once policy makers have clarified what they are trying to accomplish, it is relatively easy to determine the kind of information that reflects them best and the feasibility of collecting it.

Second: Evaluation must focus on what programs accomplish (outcomes), not on what they do (outputs) (Bayley 1996a; Eck 1992; Challenges Project 2002; VERA Institute of Justice 2003). In too many evaluations, the process is treated as if it were the product. The reason is obvious. It is much easier for agencies to audit their own activities, especially the expenditure of money, than to collect information about matters happening outside their control.

Third: Programs should not be evaluated before what is proposed can reasonably be accomplished. In general, the more ambitious the goals, the longer the time required for implementation. Conversely, the more quickly evaluations are undertaken, the less informative they are likely to be.

Fourth: To ensure that results are assessed, evaluations must be mandated as part of program authorizations (Chinchilla 2001). Administrators will not evaluate programs for which they are responsible out of the kindness of their hearts. Results are too unpredictable and therefore too risky in terms of careers and agency status. Evaluation must also be included as a component of assistance programs for another reason. Procedures must be established at the beginning of projects in order to assure that descriptive information about what is being done (inputs) is collected. If it is not, it may be lost.

Fifth: The evaluation methodologies that are considered most informative in contemporary social science are not applicable to democratic foreign assistance. It is generally recognized among social scientists that the most informative way to test the impact of policy is through randomized experimentation (National Academies of Science 2003). That is, the effects of programs should be assessed against alternatives, including no program at all, that are applied to subjects (individuals, police departments, countries) which are randomly selected. This is the "gold standard" of scientific method, and has been developed most carefully for the evaluation of medical treatments. Unfortunately, it is impossible to apply this model to the evaluation of foreign assistance because countries are the subjects being treated. Not only aren't there enough countries receiving significant aid to constitute experimental and control samples, but treating them as subjects of experimentation would be politically unacceptable as well. Moreover, the experimental-random-selection methodology can't be conclusive when applied to social life because there are so many other factors that might affect impact. As sociologist Peter Rossi has famously remarked, "[T]he expected value of any measured effect of a social program is zero."

The fundamental problem is that the most rigorous social science methodologies can't be used to evaluate country-focused assistance. Moreover, trying to do so raises the cost of evaluation without improving its informativeness. What is needed, therefore, is a methodology that is good enough within these circumstance—a methodology that is at once informative, reasonably reliable, uncomplicated, understandable to policy makers, and relatively inexpensive. There is one that fits the bill: the use of panels of observers who collectively are expert about the reforms to be achieved as well as about the countries in which reforms are undertaken. The standard for judgment would be whether changes were made that differed significantly from past practice and whether they were likely to be sustained. Observers would be given access to all documents, briefed about the objectives of the programs to be evaluated, and provided sufficient time to develop their own evaluation plan. In most cases, a team of four to five carefully chosen people from outside government would be sufficient, spending from two weeks to two months on-site abroad.

Great care would need to be taken to ensure that the observers are independent of the agencies sponsoring them. This means they must come from outside government—for-profit consultants or individuals from universities, think tanks, and professional associations. Even private persons, however, may shrink from writing critical evaluations if they become dependent on winning evaluation contracts. One solution might be to have professional organizations, such as the International Association of Chiefs of Police and American social science and area studies associations, assist in selecting panelists.

Perhaps the best example of this methodology is the evaluation conducted by the Oversight Commissioner and his staff in Northern Ireland (2000–2005). The Oversight Commissioner was created to assess progress made in implementing the recommendations of the Independent Commission on Policing in Northern Ireland, usually referred to as the Patten Commission (1999). The team of four

Canadians and four Americans—seven police officers and one civilian academic—constructed performance indicators for the 171 recommendations of the Patten Commission. In many instances the judgments were made on the basis of "best practices" in Europe and North America (Oversight Commissioner 2000). This required the team to determine whether the administrative mechanisms needed to implement recommendations were in place, largely a matter of documentation. The team then assessed whether behavior matched expectations. This was done through interviews and observations, with no attempt made to undertake original quantitative research. The team was given unrestricted access to police documents and personnel and to institutions created by the Patten Report outside the police. The Oversight Commissioner's reports, published three times a year, were accepted by police and non-police alike as being reliable, informative, and professional. Although the process of evaluation made the police anxious, as one would expect, they accepted the reports as fair and accurate. In a highly charged political atmosphere, the reports of the Oversight Commissioner provided a running evaluation of accomplishments and problems in implementing one of the most inclusive blueprints for the development of a democratic police force that has ever been written.

This kind of evaluation, I believe, would in most situations be quicker, cheaper, less burdensome, and more informative than what is normally done.

Conclusion

Providing assistance for the reform of police abroad is difficult and the benefits are hard to measure. Evidence to date does not indicate that it contributes significantly to changing the practices or enhancing the capacity of the police, although there are instances when it may have done so. There is even less evidence that reform assistance to the police contributes to the development of democratic government generally. Perhaps the best that reform assistance can achieve is, in Philip Heymann's words, a "fairly robust dialogue" with foreign officials (Heymann 1992). This should not, however, be viewed as a negligible achievement. Because foreign assistance cannot, and, on the evidence, does not, contribute to reform if local officials are not convinced of its value, robust dialogue is the essential ingredient for success. It is the first step in producing enduring change.

Existing evaluation methodologies are generally either superficial or dauntingly demanding. Nonetheless, providing reform assistance without evaluation of impact is like treating a serious physical ailment with offerings of gold coins and pious incantations. The solution is to provide *systematically* for qualitative evaluations by independent experts, based on a clear specification of the goals that reform assistance is supposed to achieve.

8

Organizing for Success

What should the U.S. government do to improve its ability to use foreign assistance to develop effective, democratic police abroad? The U.S. government should develop the voice and capacity for doing developmental criminal justice abroad, utilizing the latest understanding of best practices in crime control carefully adapted to the needs and traditions of recipient countries. This is easy to say but hard to do.

In order to determine how this can be accomplished, it is important to begin with a clear understanding of the shortcomings of current assistance efforts. The benchmarks I use for judging the adequacy of our efforts are implicit in the earlier discussions of what is needed for successful reform—substantively (chapter 4), with particular attention to the tension between law enforcement and reform (chapter 5), and tactically (chapter 6). After reviewing these shortcomings, I will make two sets of recommendations for improving performance: (1) programmatic, that is, the requirements for success

in any assistance effort regardless of agency ownership; and (2) organizational, that is, the changes that need to be made in the way in
which foreign assistance for the justice sector is organized.

Shortcomings

American government efforts to assist the development of police
abroad suffer from the following problems.

1. *Lack of accountability.* Quite simply, the U.S. government
doesn't know what it's doing with respect to police assistance, or justice assistance more generally. Although it encourages transparency
in police operations abroad, it cannot provide consolidated information about the amount and nature of its own foreign assistance to
police. This is particularly ironic because Congress expressly pro-
hibited assistance to foreign police in 1974 except under carefully
enumerated conditions. However, so many exemptions to its prohibition have been granted that oversight has virtually disappeared.
It is scattered among executive agencies and wholly lacking on the
part of Congress.

2. *Absence of strategic planning.* Currently, efforts to assist police
abroad are characterized by ad hoc programs developed without
explicit, carefully considered rationales connecting program inputs
to program goals. Police-assistance programs are determined largely
by how much money is available for such assistance and by the nature
of programs American providers are prepared to deliver. Police assistance is a supply-side exercise, based on what is available rather than
what is needed. Too often, therefore, the expenditure of money in
particular ways becomes the primary measure of success. Success,
either in terms of law-enforcement capacity or democratic institutional change, is achieved by accident rather than design.

3. *Subordination of democratic institutional reform to increasing
foreign law-enforcement capacity.* The overarching goal of American assistance to foreign police is clear—to safeguard the United
States from criminal activity emanating from abroad. Currently, the
main concerns are terrorism, narcotics, trafficking in people, money
laundering, and regulation of borders. There is growing attention
to violations of intellectual property rights and cyber-crime. These
Washington-mandated priorities have become the mantra justifying

police assistance in every country around the globe. As a result, the bulk of American assistance efforts go to raising police capacity to fight crime and maintain order with little attention given to constructing long-range plans for institutional development supporting democratic government.

At the same time, legislation authorizing police assistance requires that it either support, or at least not be at the expense of, the development of "internationally recognized standards of human rights, the rule of law, anti-corruption, and the promotion of civilian police roles that support democracy" (Foreign Assistance Act, Section 660 [b][6]). These are undoubtedly sincere expressions of American values, but in practice they have become the boundary conditions for police assistance rather than a high-priority goal. They are an afterthought rather than a programmatic priority.

4. *Overemphasis on the crime-control needs of the United States relative to those of the country being assisted.* American assistance programs not only give overwhelming priority to building law-enforcement capacity but also focus on criminal threats to the United States rather than to local populations. American police assistance is more responsive to our security needs than to theirs. Is it reasonable to expect, for example, that people abroad are as concerned with international organized crime, narcotics trafficking, international protection of property rights, and money laundering as they are in burglary, hooliganism, and robbery? American assistance seems more interested in enlisting foreign police in protecting the United States than in helping them protect their own people.

5. *Uncritical promotion of deterrent law enforcement.* Police assistance is devoted largely to enhancing the capacity of foreign governments to detect and prosecute criminal cases, particularly the types enumerated above. It is based on the theory that crime is most effectively controlled by punishment. American programs give hardly any attention to alternative strategies, such as preventive patrol, community self-defense, situational crime-prevention, target hardening, and the tactics of community- and problem-oriented policing. Our advocacy of community policing, for example, is vague and imprecise, and can be dangerous in certain contexts. The United States does give some attention to building local capacity for intelligence-gathering, especially with respect to counter-terrorism and counter-narcotics, but relatively little to improving the ability of for-

eign police to monitor and analyze patterns of ordinary crimes such as burglary, robbery, rape, and assault.

6. *Overreliance on training not embedded in programs of institutional change.* Each year, the United States offers hundreds of training courses at home and abroad involving thousands of people. Overwhelmingly, these courses are designed to enhance specialized skills relating to law enforcement. Few of them focus on management, and hardly any on serious examination of issues relating to democracy, protection of human rights, and accountability. Furthermore, because training is given as a series of discrete exercises, sometimes as a quid pro quo for law-enforcement cooperation, there is no assurance that what is learned will actually be applied. Unless the utilization of such training is foreseen and facilitated, the training is wasted. Training in strategic management, tailored to local circumstances, should be a prerequisite for investment in the development of technical and applied skills.

7. *Failure to adapt programs to local circumstances, especially those of historical tradition and practice.* American assistance planning rarely involves an assessment of the fit between American programs and local practice. Assistance is usually modeled on American practice regardless of whether it represents an improvement over what is done locally.

8. *Underappreciation of the importance of consulting and collaborating with local stakeholders.* American assistance is often offered on a take-it-or-leave-it basis rather than being negotiated as part of an ongoing discussion of institutional needs. Local police agencies are not clean slates on which Americans can write. Unless local stakeholders are invited to sit down as partners with Americans to determine needs, support for assistance may be limited to a small group of participants who benefit directly from the assistance. In order to make a sustained difference to institutional practice, support must be developed between everyone in the chain of command, especially executives who allocate resources and supervisors who reward individual performance. Assistance should be used to develop leaders within the police who are willing to commit themselves to broad institutional objectives.

9. *Inadequate numbers of expert staff to plan and implement criminal justice assistance programs.* The U.S. government has not developed a sufficient cadre of people who are skilled at formulating

developmental strategies, experienced in adapting plans to foreign conditions, and willing to be deployed quickly as needed around the world. The Department of State is staffed by generalist foreign service officers who lack expertise in professional law-enforcement; the Department of Justice (DOJ) is led by lawyers, often former prosecutors, who have little experience with overseas development; the mission of the law-enforcement agencies of DOJ, primarily the FBI and DEA, is investigation and prosecution rather than long-range development; and the U.S. Agency for International Development (USAID), although development-focused, is unskilled in policing and reluctant to become involved in police assistance. Only the International Criminal Investigative Training Assistance Program (ICITAP) and the Office of Prosecutorial Development, Assistance and Training (OPDAT), both within the Department of Justice, have the right sort of people for this task, though not in sufficient numbers to take responsibility for worldwide democratic police development or for justice stabilization and reconstruction in post-conflict situations. Unfortunately, ICITAP and OPDAT have little standing even within their own department. The Department of State, indeed, appears to value them more than the Department of Justice, which explains in part why the Department of State has made efforts to have ICITAP and OPDAT's activities transferred to it.

10. *Inability to learn from experience.* Foreign assistance in the justice sector is not designed as a "learning" operation. Evaluations are few, experience in the field is not studied systematically for "best practice," people returning from overseas missions are not debriefed for insights into improvement, and agencies do not share assistance experience. Civilian agencies operating abroad, especially those involved in development, lack the capacity to learn that has become institutionalized in the Department of Defense. Unlike the military, civilian agencies do not conduct pre-deployment exercises, give scant attention to after-operations analysis, do not systematically debrief returning personnel, and provide only superficial "action" reports. This problem is undoubtedly aggravated by reliance on NGOs and private contractors who are reluctant to submit themselves to evaluations that might expose flaws in performance.

Although the shortcomings enumerated here are real and widely acknowledged by observers, it would be a mistake to write off American assistance to foreign police and foreign justice systems as wasted. Despite these problems, a great deal of good has been done. The skills of some foreign police have been raised; essential infrastructure has been created or upgraded; issues of institutional development have been addressed in some places, such as corruption, budgetary management, accountability, and internal discipline; and training has been broadened in subject-matter and has risen in quality. Policy manuals have been developed and promulgated for critical operations, such as investigations, use of firearms, and control of public-order events. Moreover, American programs have supported the revision of laws within which police operate and have raised the quality of prosecution, adjudication, and incarceration. Finally, a small cadre of justice development specialists has been developed in OPDAT and ICITAP whose work is increasingly viewed as important.

Because almost all the money for police assistance flows through INL in the Department of State and because INL presides over the granting of exemptions under Section 660 of the Foreign Assistance Act, there is reasonable accountability, at least in principle. In addition, the Europe and Eurasia Bureau of the Department of State has created a special office to plan and coordinate all assistance, including police and justice assistance, to its region. During the Clinton administration, the Law Enforcement Interagency Working Group, composed of about twenty people representing the major law-enforcement and foreign assistance agencies, met regularly to coordinate plans, evaluate requests for funds, and generate general policy. This group was disbanded by the Bush administration.

Most important of all, people on the ground in American embassies abroad who have responsibility for implementing assistance programs seem to have a greater understanding than people in Washington of the shortcomings of existing efforts. They recognize the importance of interagency collaboration, of local long-term institutional development, of treating foreign recipients as partners, and of local knowledge. This is due in part to the scale of operations in embassies, where bureaucratic rivalries, though always present, are easier to overcome through face-to-face interaction. All embassies have a law-enforcement coordinating group under the Deputy Chief of Mission (DCM). Several have also appointed a Foreign Service Officer as security coordinator. The Department of Justice has also appointed Resident Legal Advisors, all from OPDAT, to seventeen embassies and one regional organization to assess local needs, plan assistance programs, and coordinate assistance efforts (Private communication August 2004).[1] In concert with local governments, embassies negotiate "letters of agreement" stipulating the goals of justice assistance and how the United States will contribute. Finally, the recruitment of Foreign Services Nationals from local populations, including police and security services, has improved the understanding of local practices and communication with key stakeholders.

The shortcomings in police assistance, then, should not be attributed to the quality of American personnel, but to the inadequacies of the systems within which they work. By and large, the people who implement police assistance, including those from law-enforcement agencies, are bright, knowledgeable about foreign practices, and insightful about the need for an institutional approach. They are often critical of the strategic shortcomings in American assistance efforts and understand the value of closer local consultation.

In sum, a great many concerned, intelligent, and experienced people within the U.S. government are doing the best they can within the limitations of law, structure, and bureaucratic tradition to overcome the shortcomings enumerated. But there is only so much determined individuals can do. Their dedication and good intentions need to be supported by programmatic reform and structural reorganization.

Programmatic Recommendations

Efforts to change bureaucratic performance, whether within police agencies or in governments at large, tend to focus on structural reorganization, that is, on changing the assignment of tasks among constituent units. This is a mistake. What is needed more commonly is a change in the customary way of doing business. Reforms should begin by specifying the changes in practice that are required

---

1. China, Thailand, Columbia, Nicaragua, Paraguay, Azerbaijan, Georgia, Moldova, Russia, Uzbekistan, Albania, Bosnia, Bulgarian, Kosovo, Macedonia, Romania, Serbia and Montenegro, and the Southeast European Cooperative Initiative (SECI).

to achieve improved performance in police assistance regardless of where responsibility is assigned. As in architecture, form should follow function. It follows, then, that changing the way government is organized should be undertaken only if it contributes to a change in the way in which people work.

I believe that American efforts to develop effective and humane police abroad would be improved if assistance programs, to whomever assigned, incorporated the following practices.

1. *Coherent assistance plans for every recipient country should be developed, combining the goals of both enhancing law-enforcement effectiveness and inculcating democratic practices.* No assistance program should be approved and funded unless it can be justified by an explicit process of reasoning linking assistance inputs to developmental goals in specific countries. Expert strategizing informed by local knowledge is the solution to the current ad hoc'ery in American police assistance.

2. *Assistance programs should recognize that increasing law-enforcement effectiveness and developing democratic police practices are not antithetical but mutually supporting.* This is the key "mentality" that must be changed in American police assistance. In 1968, Professor Herbert Packer said that activities of criminal justice systems could be judged from two points of view—their effectiveness at crime control and their adherence to principles of due process (Packer). He referred to these as the "crime control" and "due process" models of criminal justice. This formulation suggests a tension between the two and implies a choice to be made. Most police, in my experience, accept this, as do many of the public.

In planning assistance programs for the police, there are both substantive and tactical reasons for not acting according to the implied Packer trade-offs, but for finding ways to maximize both goals simultaneously. Substantively, the police will be more effective at preventing crime and punishing criminals if the public is willing to assist them with information and resources. In order to nurture and increase this essential input, police must demonstrate their fairness, which means adhering to recognized standards of human rights. There is also a growing body of evidence showing that people are less likely to recommit offences if they have been treated with respect and fairness by adjudicating authorities (Skogan and Frydl

2003; Tyler 1997). In other words, being democratic enhances rather than undermines the effectiveness of the police.

In this connection, terminology may be an important indicator of orientation. Foreigners often remark that American advisors refer to police *forces* rather than police *services* as Australians, Canadians, and British do. Foreigners also observe that American advisors tend to describe the goal of assistance to be the creation of professional law-enforcement, implying an emphasis on deterrence, rather than "quality service delivery" which leaves the nature of police activity to be determined locally.

There are also important tactical reasons for combining the goal of law-enforcement effectiveness with that of democratic development. The avowed purpose of the police everywhere is to provide public security. Law enforcement is what police believe they are created to do. And it is what they are universally expected to do. It is very difficult, therefore, to get their attention, let alone their enthusiasm, for institutional reform if foreign assistance does not serve this core mission. To achieve democratic policing, foreign advisors must appeal to professional self-interest.

Furthermore, because the United States is concerned with reducing criminal threats to itself from overseas, American access to foreign police agencies is often primarily through their criminal investigators. Detectives are considered elite police officers everywhere. The path to promotion often leads through this specialty, which accounts for the fact that it usually attracts the best and the brightest officers within a police service. Reform is unlikely to occur if this cadre of police officers, who are disproportionately influential in most police agencies, do not see deterrent effectiveness improve as well. This means paying attention to developing their professionalism in detection and investigation. Routine law-enforcement contacts internationally provide ready access to this strategic group of foreign police officers.

Finally, criminal investigators are often the nexus for the sort of official corruption that disillusions the public most, namely, the denial of justice due to money or influence. If eliminating corruption and instituting the rule of law are important for winning the support of the public, then reforming criminal investigations is the place to begin.

Interestingly, many Americans with experience in overseas training and assistance recognize this synergism between law-enforcement effectiveness and democratic reform. Agents of the FBI and DEA, for example, are often keenly aware that law-enforcement cooperation between the United States and foreign countries is undercut by corruption, lawlessness, unreflective and unskilled management, non-transparency, ineffective first-line supervision, and political interference. Consequently, they don't see a conflict of interest with the reform assistance activities of ICITAP and OPDAT. Nor do reform-minded people from USAID, OPDAT, and ICITAP, who are stationed overseas, report tension between their activities and those of American law-enforcement specialists.

This is not to imply, however, that the United States has devoted as much attention and resources to democratic justice reform as it has to the development of foreign law-enforcement capabilities. People concerned with human rights, especially in Latin America, have strongly criticized the U.S. government for its imbalance in investment in developing law-enforcement capacity rather than law-enforcement reform (Nield 2004; Washington Office on Latin America 1995). They contend, as do some police advisors themselves, that law-enforcement agencies are willing to exchange reform for cooperation (Royal Canadian Mounted Police 2003). Moreover, the connection between law-enforcement capacity-building and system reform is asymmetrical. Capacity building, especially of a technical sort, does little to change the quality of system activity, whereas system reform can improve the effectiveness of law enforcement.

The point is that whatever the current mix of capacity building and reform in foreign assistance, both would gain by recognizing their essential connectedness and, consequently, by being planned together.

3. *In supporting the development of more effective police abroad, U.S. assistance programs should be responsive to the needs of local populations, giving as much attention to preventive crime-control as to criminal threats to the United States.* Because a key ingredient to democratic policing, and to democratic legitimacy, is responsiveness to the safety concerns of local populations, American assistance must give as much attention to this as to its own security—if, that is, the United States is truly interested in the democratic development of policing abroad, as it so often professes to be. To this end, the

United States should encourage and support surveys of local criminal-victimization, as well as surveys of public respect for the police and experience with them. And it should support the creation of representative consultative groups to assist police in setting crime-control priorities.

4. *As a first priority, police assistance should support the development of evidence-based management.* Because the key to obtaining the cooperation of police in programs of reform is their avowed interest in becoming more effective at crime control, American assistance should place the highest priority on raising their capacity to analyze the effectiveness of what they are doing and promoting the use of such information in managing operations. In other words, we should take foreign police at their word when they say they want to become more effective law-enforcement professionals, and then insist that they collect reliable information about crime and their own activities and that they use this information to justify what they do. This is the basic premise of CompStat, New York City's much praised management tool. Police operations cannot be transparent to others if they are not transparent to themselves. And in most of the world, operational analysis of police activities either by the police or by outsiders is primitive. When it exists at all, police research tends to be theoretical rather than empirical and legalistic rather than operational. The fact is that most police agencies have no evidence that what they are doing is improving public safety despite protestations about wanting to be more effective,

In my opinion, the most powerful lever that the United States has in creating democratic policing abroad is the sponsorship of evidence-based management. This would not only provide the basis for transparency but also produce a mind-set that would open the police to discovering for themselves the value of a cooperative public, and hence, the value of fairness. It is no accident that in the United States the rise of evaluative scientific research on the police in the latter part of the 20th century coincided with the development of what some observers have called "constitutional policing," which is an amalgam of enhanced responsiveness, community consultation, accountability, and legal rectitude (Kelling and Moore 1989).

The United States has more experience using empirical research to enlighten police operations than any other country (Skogan and Frydl 2003). It is our unique contribution to modern policing, and our comparative advantage in international police assistance. It is time to deploy this capability for the benefit of police abroad.

5. *Police assistance must be based on systematic analysis of the "fit" between program recommendations and local circumstances.* The planning of foreign assistance for police abroad must take into account the compatibility between what we provide and local practice and custom. Off-the-shelf training programs, for example, are wasted if they are based entirely on American experience. This means that area experts should be involved in formulating justice programs and that resources should be made available for background research.

6. *Strategic development plans for the police must be part of a comprehensive program covering all aspects of the justice process—policing, prosecution, adjudication, and corrections—in a coordinated way.* This observation is commonplace in discussions about police assistance. The sectors of criminal justice systems are complexly interrelated, activities in one area directly effecting what happens in others. Moreover, because the process of planning and implementing police reform is very much the same across the criminal justice system, people providing assistance in one area can learn from people in another.

Organizational Recommendations

The likelihood that the six programmatic recommendations just discussed will be adopted in American assistance programs depends in large measure on whether a strategic, holistic, and developmental view of police assistance is effectively championed in the policy councils of government and whether the capacity to implement such plans is developed and coordinated. At the present time, the "voice" for these recommendations as well as the capacity to act on them is weak. The primary reason for this is that police assistance is carried out by exemption to Section 660 of the Foreign Assistance Act. There is no positive Congressional authorization for police assistance stipulating goals and assigning responsibility. As a result, Congressional oversight is fitful and responsibility for planning and implementing police assistance is not concentrated within agencies that are either developmentally focused or expert in criminal justice. I believe, therefore, that the organization of the U.S. government with respect to police and justice assistance needs to be changed. To create both voice and capacity for a coordinated developmental view of police assistance, I make two recommendations.

1. *The division of labor for justice assistance between the Department of State and the Department of Justice should be changed.* The Department of Justice should be given exclusive responsibility for planning and implementing police and justice assistance abroad. This involves assessing needs, developing assistance strategies to achieve effective and humane policing, consulting with stakeholders abroad, adapting plans to fit the particularities of local contexts, and analyzing operations for "best practices." The Department of Justice should also recruit, train, deploy, and support people sent abroad to implement assistance programs, whether into countries making peaceful transitions to democracy, into failed states emerging from civil conflict, or into countries taken over by the international community as threats to world order.

It is easier to hold one agency responsible for planning and implementing police assistance than several through the cumbersome mechanisms of interagency coordination. Although this point is widely accepted, there is sharp disagreement over which agency this should be. With the division of labor I recommend, observers would at least know who to go to in order to put things right.

Decisions about where and how much justice assistance is appropriate for particular countries would be made at senior executive levels in collaboration with Congress, guided by the advice of the State Department. The Department of State should be responsible for determining the compatibility of police and justice assistance with American foreign policy interests. It should also be given the task of evaluating the impact of justice assistance programs, working closely with a "lessons learned" unit of the Department of Justice. All foreign justice assistance should be a consolidated item in the foreign operations appropriation covering the administrative costs incurred by the Department of Justice, the operating costs of justice programs abroad, and the evaluation activities of the Department of State.

In short, I recommend that the Department of Justice become the expert body within the U.S. government that designs and implements justice assistance in peaceful as well as post-conflict situations, but under the supervision of the Department of State. The U.S. government, though it might choose not to do what DOJ recommends in particular cases, should at least be presented with the best thinking about what appropriate justice programs look like, maximizing both law enforcement and reform goals.

This does not mean that the Department of Justice should become the agency that directs and coordinates nation building as a whole when that is required. Nation building, as in Iraq or Afghanistan, might be handled respectively by a unit within the Department of State, as suggested in Senate bill 2127, by a new executive agency, by interagency coordination, or by the Department of Defense. The Department of Justice's obligation would be to contribute the justice piece to whatever stabilization and reconstruction efforts the United States engaged in, just as the Department of Defense provides military capacity, USAID economic investment, the Department of Energy expertise on essential infrastructure, and so forth. Because reconstructing effective, democratic police systems in strife-torn countries encounters the same problems of substance and tactics found in bilateral assistance in peaceful contexts, it makes sense to develop this capacity at one location in the U.S. government, making it available to other agencies and departments as required in different circumstances. Post-conflict reconstruction should be seen as a dramatic example of a generic problem, namely, how to facilitate the development abroad of effective and humane justice systems.

There are several reasons for making the Department of Justice the responsible agency for planning and implementing justice assistance.

First: Law enforcement and institutional reform, in substance and tactics, cannot be separated in practice abroad. Because the U.S. government's concern about criminal threats from abroad is legitimate and politically popular, the chances of developing a holistic, development approach to justice assistance is more likely to happen by working with DOJ than around it. Any trade-offs between capacity building and institutional reform should be decided explicitly by people sitting around the same table in the same agency.

Second: Because of its standing and expertise, the Department of Justice will have a more compelling voice within the U.S. government for reform-oriented justice assistance, especially to police, than any other agency or department.

Third: the Department of Justice already has units within it, such as ICITAP and OPDAT, that have developed the sort of programmatic approach to police and justice assistance that is needed. This sort of expertise does not exist in either the Department of State or USAID. Indeed, both agencies "outsource" to ICITAP and OPDAT for precisely this reason. It will, I believe, be easier to import a broadened developmental perspective into DOJ than to import law-enforcement and justice expertise into either the Department of State or USAID. The Department of State is not primarily an operational agency; its responsibilities are analytic and diplomatic. USAID, because of its experience with the Office of Public Safety in the 1960s and 1970s, is very reluctant to become involved with justice assistance, especially with the police. It fears contaminating its economic and social programs, especially its efforts to develop civil society.

Fourth: The operational law-enforcement agencies of DOJ, such as the FBI and DEA, already have extensive experience with foreign training. Although their efforts are narrow and technical, their overseas personnel have developed considerable insight into institutional impediments to capacity building and reform abroad. This expertise is a resource to be used. Moreover, DOJ already manages two of America's three major international police training institutions, namely, the International Law Enforcement Academies in Hungary and Thailand.

Fifth: Personnel from DOJ have access to critical stakeholders in foreign police agencies and, because they are law-enforcement professionals, have greater credibility in recommending new institutional improvements than people from other U.S. agencies.

2. *The Department of Justice must be transformed so it can carry out its new developmental responsibilities.* As currently organized and staffed, the Department of Justice cannot perform as required by this new division of labor. It has neither the inclination nor the skill to become the U.S. government's prime contractor for justice development assistance. Its primary mission is law enforcement, not institutional development; its law-enforcement orientation is toward deterrence; its focus of attention is largely domestic, becoming international only as overseas activities impinge on American security; and apart from the subordinate law-enforcement agencies, it is staffed largely by lawyers.

In order to speak authoritatively about justice development abroad and to carry it out, the Department of Justice would have to change in fundamental ways.

1. It would need to develop the capacity to strategize about crime problems of all sorts, not simply those mandated to its specialized law-enforcement agencies. It would have to marshal the experience of full-service police agencies in the United States. In order to do so, the Justice Department would need to recruit people who have experience in state and local law-enforcement in the United States. It could no longer rely almost exclusively, as it has done in the past, on federal personnel to assess, teach, and advise abroad.

It must also learn to make greater use of the knowledge about policing and crime-prevention contained in the research sponsored by its own National Institute of Justice. The knowledge that the Department of Justice needs about crime prevention and "best practices" in policing is already available. It must be used systematically to inform overseas development efforts.

2. The Department of Justice must learn to think developmentally about the connections between effective law enforcement and institutional reform. It must put experts on capacity building, on the one hand, and justice reform, on the other, in the same room to explore the benefits and difficulties of working together in coordinated programs.

3. The Department of Justice must develop a permanent corps of justice monitors, managers, teachers, and advisors that can be posted abroad. It should create a "justice foreign service," as there is a diplomatic foreign service in the Department of State and an economic and social foreign service in USAID. These professionals would be assigned both to DOJ in Washington and to embassies around the world to help coordinate assistance in the field, very much as Resident Legal Officers do now.

In addition, the Department of Justice should assume responsibility for recruiting and training a ready reserve of police and other justice advisors that can be deployed abroad on short notice in failed and conflicted states to provide instant and meaningful public safety and access to justice.

4. The Department of Justice should search constantly for "best practices" in police assistance, paying particular attention to the lessons learned by its own personnel abroad. Evaluation and debriefing

of assistance programs must be undertaken systematically and the findings shared widely.

In order to manage all these new responsibilities, the Department of Justice should create a Division of International Development, headed by an Assistant Attorney-General. At the present time, there is an Office of International Affairs within the Criminal Division, which supervises OPDAT and ICITAP. This office should become its own division, highlighting the new prominence of overseas development in the DOJ portfolio. It would coordinate the overseas assistance work of all agencies and units within the Department of Justice.

Conclusion

The major benefits of this reorganization of responsibilities within the U.S. government is twofold: it lodges responsibility for police assistance in all foreign contexts in one place and it brings together all of the government's overseas practitioners, and hence expertise, in justice development. The Department of Justice has potentially both the voice and capacity, as no other government department and agency does, to raise the level of performance in providing assistance for effective democratic police around the world. In order to do this, however, the Department of Justice must itself change, accepting the new mandate and developing the capacity to perform accordingly.

In short, if the U.S. government is genuinely committed to developing democratic police abroad, it must put all the required expertise in its foremost justice agency, appropriately supervised by its foremost foreign policy agency. In that way, structural confusion will no longer be an excuse for programmatic failure. If the Department of Justice cannot perform as needed, then it must be reshaped so that it can. In order to be successful in producing democratic reform in justice institutions abroad, the American government must itself be willing to change. Reform abroad begins with reform at home.

Appendix: Executive Summary of Recommendations

I. Democracy criteria

1. Police must be accountable to law rather than to government.
2. Police must protect human rights, especially those rights that are required for the sort of unfettered political activity that is the hallmark of democracy.
3. Police must be accountable to people outside their organizations who are specifically designated and empowered to regulate police activity.
4. Police must give top operational priority to servicing the needs of individual citizens and private groups.

II. Strategies of reform assistance

1. Provide a legal basis for the new police.
2. Create specialized, independent oversight of the police.

3. Staff the police with the right sort of people.
4. Develop the capacity of police executives to manage reform.
5. Focus on the safety needs of individuals.
6. Require legality and fairness in all actions.

Do not rely on:

1. Generalized training
2. Organizational restructuring
3. Material support.

III. Balancing security and reform

1. Priority should be given to developing the capacity of police forces to manage by results.
2. Offers of foreign assistance should be contingent on local police implementing the four specified democratic reforms: rule of law, human rights, accountability, and responsiveness.
3. Assistance designed to build law-enforcement capacity should not be given unless that capacity is to be used as part of an explicit and defensible crime-control strategy.
4. Foreign assistance should be given primarily for addressing the security needs articulated by individuals rather than those articulated by governments.
5. Countries that provide assistance to foreign police should place local security needs, especially those of the general population, ahead of their own.
6. Foreign police assistance should create demonstrable crime-control "wins" as rapidly as possible.
7. Foreign assistance should be used to encourage local police to concentrate their crime prevention and control efforts on their country's poor.

IV. Tactics of reform assistance

1. Develop a comprehensive plan.
2. Prepare for the long haul.
3. Adapt reform plans to local conditions.
4. Persuade local stakeholders to support reform.
5. Treat aid recipients as partners.

6. Coordinate assistance efforts.
7. Send the right people into the field.

V. Improving U.S. government performance

A. Programmatic

1. Coherent assistance plans for every recipient country should be developed, combining the goals of both enhancing law-enforcement effectiveness and inculcating democratic practices.
2. Assistance programs should recognize that increasing law-enforcement effectiveness and developing democratic police practices are not antithetical but mutually supporting.
3. In supporting the development of more effective police abroad, U.S. assistance programs should be responsive to the needs of local populations, giving as much attention to preventive crime-control as to criminal threats to the United States.
4. As a first priority, police assistance should support the development of evidence-based management.
5. Police assistance must be based on systematic analysis of the "fit" between program recommendations and local circumstances.
6. Strategic development plans for the police must be part of a comprehensive program covering all aspects of the justice process—policing, prosecution, adjudication, and corrections—in a coordinated way.

B. Organizational

1. The division of labor for justice assistance between the Department of State and the Department of Justice should be changed.
2. The Department of Justice must be transformed so it can carry out its new developmental responsibilities.

Bibliography

Annan, K. 1998. "Stop Blaming Colonialism, UN Chief Tells Africa." *New York Times*, April 17, sec. A3.

Australian Agency for International Development. *Aid Budget Summary, 2002–2003*. Canberra, Australia: AAID.

Ball, Nicole. 2001. "Transforming Security Sectors: The IMF and World Bank Approaches." *Journal of Conflict, Security and Development* 1 (7): 45–66.

Barkan, J. D. 1997. "Can Established Democracies Nurture Democracy Abroad? Lessons from Africa." In *Democracy's Victory and Crisis*, ed. A. Hadenius. Cambridge: Cambridge University Press.

Bayley, David H. 1964. *Public Liberties in the New States*. Chicago: Rand McNally.

———. 1975. "The Police and Political Development in Europe." In *The Formation of National States in Europe*, ed. Charles Tilley. Princeton, NJ: Princeton University Press.

———. 1977. "The Limits of Police Reform." In *The Police and Society*, ed. David H. Bayley. Beverly Hills, CA: Sage.

———. 1985. *Patterns of Policing*. New Brunswick, NJ: Rutgers University Press.

———. 1989. *A Model of Community Policing: The Singapore Story*. Washington, DC: National Institute of Justice.

———. 1991. *Forces of Order: Policing Modern Japan*. Berkeley: University of California Press.

———. 1994. *The Future of Policing*. New York: Oxford University Press.

———. 1996a. "Measuring Overall Effectiveness." Chap. 3 in *Quantifying Quality in Policing*, ed. Larry Hoover. Washington, DC: Police Executive Research Forum.

———. 1996b. "Police Brutality Abroad." Chap. 14 in *Police Violence: Understanding and Controlling Police Abuse of Force*, ed. William A. Geller and Hans Toch. New Haven, CT: Yale University Press.

———. 1997. "Who Are We Kidding? or Developing Democracy through Police Reform." In *Policing in Emerging Democracies*, ed. U.S. National Institute of Justice and the Bureau of International Narcotics and Law Enforcement Affairs, U.S. Department of State, 59–64. Washington, DC: U.S. Department of Justice.

———. 2001. *Democratizing the Police Abroad: What to Do and How to Do It*. Washington, DC: National Institute of Justice.

———. 2002. "Law Enforcement and the Rule of Law: Is There a Trade-off?" *Criminology and Public Policy* 2 (1): 133–154.

Bayley, David H., and Jerome H. Skolnick. 1986. *The New Blue Line*. New York: The Free Press.

Beidas, S., Colin Granderson, and Rachel Neild. 2003. "Intervention and Institution Building in Haiti." In *Constructing Security and Justice After War*, ed. Thomas J. Watson Institute for International Studies and the U.S. Institute of Peace. Washington, DC: U.S. Institute of Peace.

Bentley, D., and R. Oakley. 1995. "Peace Operations: A Comparison of Somalia and Haiti." In *Strategic Forum*, ed. Institute for National Strategic Studies. Washington, DC: National Defense University.

Berkow, M. 1999. "Practical Issues in Providing Police Assistance Abroad." In *Civilian Police and Multinational Peacekeeping— A Workshop Series: A Role for Democratic Policing*, ed. J. Burack, W. Lewis, and E. Marks, 11–16. Washington, DC: Center for Strategic and International Studies and the Police Executive Forum.

Biebesheimer, C. 1999. "Justice Reform in Latin America and the Caribbean: The IDB Perspective." Paper presented at the conference on "International Organizations, NGOs, and Rule of Law Construction: Issues in Judicial Reform in Latin America." London: Institute of Latin American Studies.

Blair, A., and M. J. Dziedzic. 1997. "The International Police Task Force." In *Lessons from Bosnia*, ed. L. Wentz, 139–166. Washington, DC: U.S. Department of Defense.

Blair, A., and M. J. Dziedzic. 1997. "Peacekeeping and Policing in Bosnia." In *Policing the New World Disorder*, ed. R. Oakley, M. Dziedzic, and E. M. Goldberg. Washington, DC: National Defense University, Institute for Strategic Studies.

Blair, H., and G. Lansen. 1994. *Weighing In on the Scales of Justice: Strategic Approaches for Donor-Supported Rule of Law Programs.* Washington, DC: U.S. Agency for International Development.

Boisvert, L., Ivan Menard, and Jean Ostiguy. 2000. *Challenges of Public Security Activities in a Post-Conflict Situation Based on the Case of Haiti.* Ottawa: Canadian International Development Agency (CIDA).

Boydstun, J. E., and M. E. Sherry. 1975. *San Diego Community Profile: Final Report.* Washington, DC: Police Foundation, National Institute of Justice.

Brahmi Report. 2000. *Report of the Panel on United Nations Peace Operations.* New York: United Nations.

Braithwaite, John. 1989. *Crime, Shame, and Integration.* Cambridge: Cambridge University Press.

Braithwaite, John, and Valerie Braithwaite. 1995. "The Politics of Legalism: Rules versus Standards in Nursing-Home Regulation." *Social and Legal Studies* 4: 307–341.

Brock, Karen, and Robert Chambers. 2001. *Consultations with the Poor: World Development Report 2000/2001.* Sussex, UK: Institute for Development Studies.

Brogden, M. 2002. "Implanting Community Policing in South Africa: A Failure of History, of Context, and of Theory." Unpublished manuscript.

Bruce, David. 2003a. "Democratic Reform of Police—Any Lessons for Kenya from South Africa?" Unpublished manuscript, Johannesburg, South Africa, Center for the Study of Violence and Reconciliation.

Bruce, David. 2003b. "New Wine from an Old Cask? The South African Police Service and the Process of Transformation." Unpublished manuscript, Johannesburg, South Africa.

Bureau of Diplomatic Security. 2002. *FY 2002 Annual Report.* http://www.diplomaticsecurity.org/library/annualrpt/pdf/FY2002AnnualReport.pdf.

Burgreen, B., and N. McPherson. 1990. "Implementing POP: The San Diego Experience." *Police Chief* 57 (10): 50.

Byrne, H., W. Stanley, and R. Garst. 2000. *Rescuing Police Reform: A Challenge for the New Guatemalan Government.* Washington DC: Washington Office on Latin America.

Call, C. 1997. "Institutional Learning within the U.S. International Criminal Investigation Training Assistance Program." In *Policing the New World Disorder,* ed. R. Oakley, M. Dziedzic, and E. M. Goldberg, 177–218. Washington, DC: National Defense University, Institute for Strategic Studies.

———. 1999a. "From Soldiers to Cops: War Transitions and the Demilitarization of Policing in Latin America and the Caribbean." PhD dissertation, Stanford University.

———. 1999b. "Sustainable Development in Central America: The Challenges of Violence, Injustice and Insecurity." Hamburg: Institut für Iberoamerika-Kunde 2000 (CA 2020: Working Paper #8).

Call, C. T. 2003. "Democratization, War and State-Building: Constructing the Rule of Law in El Salvador." *Journal of Latin American Studies* 35 (4): 1–30.

Call, C. T., and W. Stanley. 2001. "Protecting the People: Public Security Choices after Civil War." *Global Governance* 7 (April–June): 2.

Canadian International Development Agency. 2002. *Statistical Report on Official Development Assistance, FY 2001–2002.* Ottawa, Canada.

Caparini, M., and Otwin Marenin, eds. 2004. *Transforming the Police in Eastern and Central Europe.* Somerset, NJ: Transaction Publishers.

Carnegie Commission on Preventing Deadly Violence. 1995. *Promoting Democracy in the 1990s: Actors and Instruments, Issues and Imperatives.* Report of the Commission written by Larry Diamond. New York: Carnegie Corporation of New York.

Carothers, Thomas. 1999a. "The Many Agendas of Rule of Law Reform in Latin America." Paper presented at the conference on "International Organizations, NGOs, and Rule of Law Construction: Issues in Judicial Reform in Latin America." London, Institute of Latin American Studies.

Carothers, Thomas. 1999b. *Aiding Democracy Abroad: The Learning Curve.* Washington, DC: Carnegie Endowment for International Peace.

Central Intelligence Agency. 1997. "Statement of the Director of Central Intelligence Regarding the Disclosure of the Aggregate Intelligence Budget for Fiscal Year 1997." Press release, October 15.

Challenges Project and the Swedish National Defense College. 2002. *Challenges of Peace Operations: Into the 21st Century.* Stockholm, Sweden: Challenges Project and the Swedish National Defense College.

Chatterton, M. R. 1993. "Targeting Community Beat Officers: Organizational Constraints and Resistance." *Policing and Society* 3 (3): 189–204.

Cherniss, Cary. 1980. *Professional Burnout in Human Service Organizations.* New York: Praeger.

Chinchilla, L. 2001. "From Justice Reform to Public Security: Challenges for AID Agencies." Speech given at a seminar sponsored by the Washington Office on Latin America, November 2001. Washington, DC.

Clegg, Ian, Robert Hunt, and Jim Whetton. 2000. *Police Guidance on Support to Policing in Developing Countries.* Swansea: Centre for Development Studies, University of Wales.

Cochran, John K., and Mitchell B. Chamlin. 2000. "Deterrence and Brutalization: The Dual Effects of Executions." *Justice Quarterly* 17 (4): 685–706.

Cohen, L. E., M. Felson, and K. C. Land. 1983. "Property Crime in the United States: A Macrodynamic Analysis." *American Journal of Sociology* 86: 90–118.

Cohen, J. M., and J. R. Wheeler. 1997. "Training and Retention in African Public Sectors: Capacity Building Lessons for Kenya." In *Getting Good Government: Capacity Building in the Public Sectors of Developing Countries,* ed. M. S. Grindle. Cambridge, MA: Harvard Institute for International Development.

Commission on Post-Conflict Reconstruction. 2003. *Play to Win: Final Report of the Bi-Partisan Commission on Post-Conflict Reconstruction.* Washington, DC: Center for Strategic and International Affairs and the Association of the U.S. Army.

Cordone, C. 1999. "Police Reform and Human Rights Investigations: The Experience of the UN Mission in Bosnia and Herzegovina." *International Peacekeeping* 6 (4): 191–209.

Costa, G. 1995. "The United Nations and Reform of the Police in El Salvador." *International Peacekeeping* 2: 365–390.

Cottam, M. L., and O. Marenin. 1989. "Predicting the Past: Reagan Administration Assistance to Police Forces in Latin America." *Justice Quarterly* 6 (4): 589–618.

Council of Europe. 2001. *European Code of Police Ethics.* Strasbourg, France.

Couper, D. C., and S. H. Lobitz. 1991. *Quality Policing: The Madison Experience.* Washington, DC: Police Executive Research Forum, National Institute of Justice.

Covey, J. 2003. "The Custodian of the Peace Process." Draft chapter for a book edited by M. Dziedzic for the U.S. Institute of Peace Press.

Crosette, B. 2000. "The UN's Unhappy Lot: Perilous Police Duties Multiplying." *New York Times,* February 22, sec. A3.

Currie, Elliot. 1985. *Confronting Crime.* New York: Pantheon Books.

Democratization Policy Institute. 2002. "An Agenda for Bosnia's Next High Representative." Washington, DC.

Department for International Development. 2000. *Safety, Security, and Accessible Justice.* London: DFIP.

———. 2001. *Nigeria Access to Justice Programme, 2001–2008.* Lagos, Nigeria: DFIP.

———. 2002a. *Safety, Security, and Accessible Justice: Putting Policy into Practice.* London: DFIP.

———. 2002b. "Understanding and Supporting Security Sector Reform." London: DFIP.

———. 2003. *Departmental Report 2002, 2003.* London: DFIP.

Diamond, L. 1995. *Promoting Democracy in the 1990s: Actors and Instruments, Issues and Imperatives.* New York: Carnegie Corporation of New York.

Drug Enforcement Administration. 2002. Information privately supplied.

Dwan, R. 2002. *Executive Policing: Enforcing the Law in Peace Operations.* Oxford: Oxford University Press.

Eck, John E. 1992. "Helpful Hints for the Tradition-Bound Chief." *Fresh Perspectives.* Washington, DC: Police Executive Research Forum, June.

Eck, John E., and Edward R. Maguire. 2000. "Have Changes in Policing Reduced Violent Crime? An Assessment of the Evidence." Unpublished manuscript.

Fallows, James. 2004. "Blind into Baghdad." *The Atlantic*, January/February.

Foundation Center. 2002. *Summary of Domestic and International Grant Dollars, 2000*. New York: Foundation House.

Freedom House. 2002. "Freedom in the World 2002: The Annual Survey of Political Rights and Civil Liberties." http://www.freedom house .org/research/freeworld/2002/index.html.

Goldsmith, A. 1995. "Democratization and Criminal Justice: Human Rights and Police Reform in Colombia." Unpublished draft.

———. 2000. "Police Accountability Reform in Columbia: The Civilian Oversight Experiment." In *Civilian Oversight of Policing: Governance, Democracy, and Human Rights*, ed. A. Goldsmith and C. Lewis, 167–194. Oxford: Hart Publishing.

Goldstein, Herman. 1990. *Problem Oriented Policing*. Philadelphia: Temple University Press.

———. 1993. "The New Policing: Confronting Complexity." In *Research in Brief*. Washington, DC: National Institute of Justice.

Golub, S. 2003. *Beyond Rule of Law Orthodoxy: The Legal Empowerment Alternative*. Washington, DC: Carnegie Endowment for International Peace.

Gray, A., and M. Manwaring. 1998. "Panama: Operation Just Cause." In *Policing the New World Disorder*, ed. R. Oakley, M. Sziedzic, and E. M. Goldberg, 3–32. Washington, DC: National Defense University, Institute for Strategic Studies.

Gray, John. 1993. *Post-Liberalism: Studies in Political Thought*. London: Routledge.

Greene, J. R. 1998. "Evaluating Planned Change Strategies in Modern Law Enforcement: Implementing Community-Based Policing." In *How to Recognize Good Policing: Problems and Issues*, ed. J. P. Brodeur, 141–160. Thousand Oaks, CA: Police Executive Research Forum and Sage.

Greenwood, Peter W., Joan Petersilia, and Jan Chaiken. 1977. *The Criminal Investigation Process*. Lexington, MA: D. C. Heath.

Gregory, F. 1996. "The United Nations Provision of Policing Services (CIVPOL) with the Framework of 'Peacekeeping' Operations: An Analysis of the Issues." *Policing and Society* 6: 145–162.

Gurr, T. R., Monty G. Marshall, and Deepak Khosla. 2001. *Peace and Conflict 2001: A Global Survey of Armed Conflicts, Self-Determination Movements, and Democracy.* College Park: Center for International Development and Conflict Management, Department of Government and Politics, University of Maryland.

Haberfield, M. R. 1997. "Poland: 'The Police Are Not the Public and the Public Are Not the Police': Transformation from Militia to Police." *Policing* 20 (4): 641–654.

Hansen, A. S. 2002a. "Strengthening Indigenous Police Capacity and the Rule of Law in the Balkans." In *Managing Security Challenges in Post-Conflict Peace-Building,* ed. M. Pugh. Boulder, CO: Lynne Rienner.

Hansen, A. S. 2002b. *From Congo To Kosovo: Civilian Police in Peace Operations.* London: International Institute for Strategic Studies.

Harlan, J. P. 1997. "The German Police: Issues in the Unification Process." *Policing* 20 (3): 532–554.

Hartz, H. A., and Laura Mercean. 2005. "Institutionalizing the Rule of Law." In *The Quest for Viable Peace,* ed. Jock Covey, Michael Dziedzic, and Leonard Hawley. Washington, DC: U.S. Institute of Peace Press.

Heymann, Philip B. 1992. "Creating Democratic Law Enforcement Institutions in Eastern Europe, Latin America, and South Africa." Unpublished essay. Quoted in Otwin Marenin, 1998, "The Goal of Democracy in International Assistance Programs." *Policing* 21 (1): 159–177.

Hilderbrand, M. E., and M. S. Grindle. 1997. "Building Sustainable Capacity in the Public Sector: What Can Be Done?" In *Getting Good Government: Capacity Building in the Public Sectors of Developing Countries,* ed. M. S. Grindle. Cambridge, MA: Harvard Institute for International Development.

Hirsch, J. L., and R. B. Oakley. 1995. *Somalia and Operation Restore Hope: Reflections on Peacemaking and Peacekeeping.* Washington, DC: U.S. Institute of Peace Press.

Holm, T. T., and Espen Barth Eide, eds. 1999. "Peacebuilding and Police Reform." *International Peacekeeping* (special issue).

Huggins, M. K. 1998. *Political Policing: The United States and Latin America.* Durham, NC: Duke University Press.

Human Rights Watch, National Coalition for Haitian Rights, and Washington Office on Latin America. 1997. *The Human Rights*

Record of the Haitian National Police. Washington, DC: Human Rights Watch.

Huntington, Samuel P. 1968. *Political Order in Changing Societies.* New Haven, CT: Yale University Press.

Ignatieff, M. 2002. "Nation-Building Lite." *New York Times Magazine,* July 28, 26ff.

Independent Commission on Policing for Northern Ireland. 1999. *A New Beginning: Policing in Northern Ireland.* Belfast, Northern Ireland: Her Majesty's Stationery Office (HSMO).

Independent Commission on the Los Angeles Police Department (Christopher Commission). 1991. *Report.* Los Angeles, CA: By the Independent Commission.

Interagency Working Group on U.S. Government-Sponsored International Exchanges and Training. 1998. *FY 1998 Annual Report.* Washington, DC: IAWG.

———. 2002, 2003. *Annual Report.* Washington, DC: IAWG.

International Association of Peacekeeping Training Centres. 1999. *International Civilian Police Training Guide.* Nova Scotia, Canada: Canadian Peacekeeping Press.

International Criminal Investigative Training Assistance Program. 1999. *Year-End Review: A Compilation of Project Descriptions.* Washington, DC: Department of Justice.

International Crisis Group. 2002. *Policing the Police in Bosnia: A Further Reform Agenda.* Sarajevo/Brussels: ICG.

Japan International Cooperation Agency. 2001. Information privately supplied.

Kamisar, Yale. 1964. "On the Tactics of Police-Prosecution Oriented Critics of the Courts." *Cornell Law Quarterly* 49: 436–477.

Kaplan, R. D. 1998. "Sometimes, Autocracy Breeds Freedom." *New York Times,* op-ed, June 28.

Kelling, G. L., and W. J. Brattan. 1993. "Implementing Community Policing: The Administration Problem." *Perspectives in Policing,* no. 17 (July). Washington, DC: National Institute of Justice.

Kelling, G. L., and C. M. Coles. 1996. *Fixing Broken Windows: Restoring Order and Reducing Crime in Our Communities.* New York: The Free Press.

Kelling, George L., and Mark H. Moore. 1989. "From Political to Reform to Community: The Evolving Strategy of Police." In *Com-*

munity Policing: Real or Rhetoric, ed. J. R. Greene and S. D. Mastrofski. Westport, CT: Praeger.

Kelly, R. W. 1997. "American Law Enforcement Perspectives on Policing in Emerging Democracies." In *Policing in Emerging Democracies: Workshop Papers and Highlights*, 25–28. Washington, DC: U.S. Department of Justice, Office of Justice Programs.

Kennan, G. F. 1995. "On American Principles." *Foreign Affairs* 74 (2): 116–126.

Kissinger, Henry. 1965. *Problems of National Strategy: A Book of Readings*. New York: Praeger.

Klein, Jacques Paul. 2001. "Democratic Control of Policing and Security Sector Reform." In *Workshop on Democratic Control of Policing and Security Sector Reform*. Geneva: Centre for the Democratic Control of Armed Forces, Nov. 1–2, 2001.

Koci, A. 1998. "Reform of the Police in Hungary and Lithuania: Empirical Findings on the Policing of Public Order." *Innovation: The European Journal of Social Sciences* 11 (3): 304–314.

Komer, Robert W. 1975. *A Systems Analysis View of the Vietnam War, 1965–72*. Vol. 9. Washington, DC: Office, Assistant Secretary of Defense for Systems Analysis.

Konz, P. 1999. "The UNDP Justice Programme in Latin America and the Caribbean: Areas of Intervention." Unpublished paper.

Leggett, T. 2001. "Crime as a Development Issue." In *Seminar Report: Crime and Policing in Transitional Societies*, ed. South African Institute of International Affairs, 8:141–150. Johannesburg, South Africa: Konrad-Adenauer-Stiftung.

Levitt, Steven D. 1994. "Using Electoral Cycles in Police Hiring to Estimate the Effect of Police on Crime." Unpublished paper.

Lewis, B., and E. Marks. 2000. "The Rule of Law in a Disorderly World: The Need for Innovation and Focus Forward." Draft paper, Washington, DC, Center for Security and International Studies.

Lewis, William, Edward Marks, and Robert Perito. 2002. *Enhancing International Civilian Police Operations*. Washington, DC: U.S. Institute of Peace.

Lipset, Seymour Martin. 1963. *The First New Nation*. New York: Basic Books.

Manning, P. K. 1992. "Information Technologies and the Police." In *Modern Policing*, ed. M. Tonry and N. Morris, 349–398. Chicago: University of Chicago Press.

Marenin, Otwin. 1998. "United States Police Assistance in Emerging Democracies." *Policing and Society* 8 (2): 153–168.

———. 1999. "The Internationalization of Democratic Policing." Unpublished manuscript, from a presentation at the annual conference of the American Society of Criminology. Washington, DC, November.

Marks, M. 1997. "Changing Police, Policing Change." *Society in Transition* 28: 54–69.

———. 2002. "Transforming Robocops? A Case Study of Police Organizational Change in the Durban Public Order Police Unit." PhD dissertation, University of Natal, Durban, South Africa.

Marotta, F. 1999. "The Blue Flame and the Gold Shield: Methodology, Challenges and Lessons Learned on Human Rights Training for Police." *Peacekeeping* 6 (4): 69–92.

Marshall, Monty G., and Keith Jaggers. 2002. *Polity IV Country Reports*. College Park: University of Maryland. http://www.cidcm.umd.edu/inscr/polity/report.htm.

Martinez, J., and E. Amaya. 2000. "The Development and Current State of El Salvador's National Civilian Police Force." Unpublished paper for Washington Office on Latin America workshop. El Salvador, 2000.

Mastrofski, S. D. 1999. *Policing for People*. Washington, DC: Police Foundation, National Institute of Justice.

McDonald, Phyllis P. 2001. *Managing Police Operations: Implementing the New York Crime Control Model—CompStat*. Belmont, CA: Wadsworth.

McHugh, H. 1994. *Key Issues in Police Training: Lessons Learned from USAID Experience*. Washington, DC: U.S. Agency for International Development.

Mobekk, E. 2002. "Policing from Below: Community Policing as an Objective in Peace Operations." In *Executive Policing: Enforcing the Law in Peace Operations*, ed. R. Dwan, 53–66. Oxford: Oxford University Press.

Monk, R. 2001. *First Preliminary Report on a Follow-On Mission to UNMIBH and the UN International Police Task Force*. Vienna, Austria: Organization for Security and Co-operation in Europe.

Monk, Richard, Tor Tanke Holm, and Serge Rumin. 2001. *Report on a Police Follow-On Mission to UNMIBH and the UN International Police Task Force*. Vienna, Austria: Organization for Security and Co-operation in Europe.

Moore, Barrington, Jr. 1967. *The Social Origins of Dictatorship and Democracy*. Boston: Beacon Press.

Moore, Mark H. 1997. *Creating Public Value: Strategic Management in Government*. Cambridge, MA: Harvard University Press.

Moore, Mark H., David Thacher, Francis X. Hartmann, and Catherine Coles. 1999. *Case Studies of the Transformation of Police Departments: A Cross-Site Analysis*. Washington, DC: The Urban Institute Press.

Myall, James. 1996. *The New Interventionism, 1991–1994*. Cambridge: Cambridge University Press.

Nadelman, Ethan A. 1997. "The Americanization of Global Law Enforcement: The Diffusion of American Tactics and Personnel." Chap. 7 in *Crime and Law Enforcement in the Global Village*, ed. William F. McDonald, 123–138. Cincinnati, OH: Anderson.

Nagin, Daniel. 1998. "Criminal Deterrence Research Data at the Onset of the Twenty-First Century." In *Crime and Justice: An Annual Review of Research*, ed. Michael Tonry. Chicago: Chicago University Press.

National Academies of Science. 2003. Workshop on Improving Evaluation of Anti-Crime Programs. September 5–6, Washington, DC.

Neild, Rachel. 1995. *Policing Haiti: Preliminary Assessment of the New Civilian Security Force*. Washington, DC: Washington Office on Latin America.

———. 1996. "Police Reform in Haiti: The Challenge of Demilitarizing Public Order and Establishing Rule of Law." Paper for conference "Governance in Haiti: Strengthening the State and Democratic Development," Ottawa, Canada, November 7–8.

———. 1998a. *Community Policing*. Police Reform Issues Packet, Section V. Washington, DC: Washington Office on Latin America.

———. 1998b. "Internal Controls and Disciplinary Units." Draft, Sect. III of larger report, Washington Office on Latin America, Washington, DC.

———. 1998c. "Police Recruitment." In *Themes and Debates in Public Security Reform: A Manual for Civil Society*. Washington, DC: Washington Office on Latin America.

———. 1999. "From National Security to Citizen Security: Civil Society and the Evolution of Public Order Debates." Draft paper, August.

———. 2001. "ICITAP and Congressional Oversight of U.S. Assistance for Foreign Police." Memorandum, Washington Office on Latin America, Washington, DC.

———. 2002. *Sustaining Reform: Democratic Policing in Central America.* Washington, DC: Washington Office on Latin American.

———. 2004. "U.S. Police Assistance and Anti-Narcotics Policies in Latin America." Draft paper.

Norwegian Agency for International Cooperation. 2001. *Annual Report.* Oslo, Norway: Norwegian Agency for International Cooperation.

Oakley, R. B., M. J. Dziedzic, and E. M. Goldberg, eds. 1998. *Policing the New World's Disorder: Peace Operations and Public Security.* Washington, DC: National Defense University.

Oettmeier, T., and L. Brown. 1988. *Community Policing: Rhetoric or Reality,* ed. J. R. Greene and S. D. Mastrofski, 121–134. New York: Praeger.

Office of Development Evaluation and Information. 2004. "USAID Loans and Grants, Obligations and Loan Authorizations." U.S. Agency for International Development. http://qesdb.cdie.org/gbk/index.html.

Oversight Commissioner. 2000 (September). *Report 1.* Belfast, Northern Ireland: Office of the Oversight Commissioner.

Oversight Commissioner. 2001–2005. *Reports 2–17.* Belfast, Northern Ireland: Office of the Oversight Commissioner.

Packer, Herbert. 1968. *The Limits of the Criminal Sanction.* Stanford, CA: Stanford University Press. See esp. chap. 8.

Perito, Robert M. 2000. "The Role of Police in Peace Operations." Master's thesis, George Mason University, Fairfax County, VA.

———. 2001. "A Critique of the OHR Report on a Police Follow-On Mission to UNMIBH and the UN International Police Task Force." Unpublished paper.

———. 2002. *The American Experience with Police in Peace Operations.* Clementsport, Nova Scotia: Pearson Peacekeeping Centre.

———. 2003. *Where Is the Lone Ranger when We Need Him? America's Search for a Peacekeeping Constabulary.* Washington, DC: U.S. Institute of Peace.

Peterson, Ruth D., and William C. Bailey. 1991. "Murder and Punishment in the Evolving Context of the Post-Furman Era." *Social Forces* 66 (3): 685–706.

———. 2003. "Is Capital Punishment an Effective Deterrent for Murder? An Examination of Social Science Research." In *America's Experiment with Capital Punishment: Reflections on the Past, Present, and Future of the Ultimate Penal Sanction,* 2nd edition, ed. James

R. Acker, Robert M. Bohm, and Charles S. Lanier. Durham, NC: Carolina Academic Press.

Phillips, Emma, Todd Fogelson, Cecilia Ales, and Gustavo Palmieri. 2003. "Common Ground and Crosscutting Themes on Funding Public Security Initiatives in Latin America." New York: VERA Institute of Justice.

Pirnie, B. R. 1998. *Civilians and Soldiers: Achieving Better Coordination.* Santa Monica, CA: Rand, National Security Research Division, Police Executive Research Forum.

Popkin, M. 1999. "Building the Rule of Law in the Context of a Peace Process: The Role of Negotiating Parties, Civil Society and the International Community." Unpublished paper.

President's Commission on Law Enforcement and Administration of Justice. 1967. *Task Force Report: The Police.* Washington, DC: U.S. Government Printing Office.

Rosa de Leon-Escribano, C. 2000. "Analysis of Police Reform in Guatemala." Workshop, Washington office on Latin America. Unpublished paper.

Rosenau, W. 1995. "Peace Operations, Emergency Law Enforcement, and Constabulary Forces." In *Peace Operations: Developing an American Strategy.* Washington, DC: National Defense University Press.

Royal Canadian Mounted Police. 2003. *International Integrated Service Delivery.* Internal document.

Sampson, R. J. 1987. "Urban Black Violence: The Effect of Joblessness and Family Disruption." *American Journal of Sociology* 93: 348–382.

Scheye, E. 2002. "Transitions to Local Authority." In *Executive Policing: Enforcing the Law in Peace Operations,* 102–123, ed. R. Dwan. Oxford: Oxford University Press.

Schmidl, E. A. 1998. "Police Functions in Peace Operations: An Overview." In *Policing the New World Disorder,* xiv–xxix, ed. R. B. Oakley, M. J. Dziedzic, and E. M. Goldberg. Washington, DC: National Defense University.

Schoenhaus, R. M. 2002. *Training for Peace and Humanitarian Operations: Advancing Best Practices.* Washington, DC: U.S. Institute of Peace.

Serafino, Nina. 2004. *Policing in Peacekeeping and Related Stability Operations: Problems and Proposed Solutions.* Congressional Research Service (CRS) Report for Congress. Washington, DC: CRS.

Sherman, Lawrence W. 1998. *Preventing Crime: What Works, What Doesn't, What's Promising.* Washington, DC: National Institute of Justice.

Sismanidis, R. D. V. 1997. *Police Functions in Peace Operations: Report from a Workshop Organized by the U.S. Institute of Peace.* Washington, DC: U.S. Institute of Peace. Series "Peaceworks No. 14."

Skogan, Westley G. 1990. *Disorder and Decline.* New York: The Free Press.

Skogan, Westley, and Kathleen Frydl, eds. 2004. *Fairness and Effectiveness in Policing: The Evidence.* Washington, DC: The National Academies Press.

Smith, T. 1994. *America's Mission: The United States and the Worldwide Struggle for Democracy in the Twentieth Century.* Princeton, NJ: Princeton University Press.

Snow, Thomas. 1997. "Competing National and Ethical Interests in the Fight against Transnational Crime: A U.S. Practitioners Perspective." Chap. 10 in *Crime and Law Enforcement in the Global Village,* ed. W. F. McDonald, 169–186. Cincinnati, OH: Anderson Publishing Company.

South African Police Service. n.d. *Co-Operation Belgian Gendarmerie and South African Police Service: Evaluation Report.* Pretoria, South Africa: South African Police Service.

Sparrow, M., H. Moore, and D. Kennedy. 1990. *Beyond 911: A New Era for Policing.* New York: Basic Books.

Stanley, W. 1993. *Risking Failure: The Problems and Promises of the New Civilian Police in El Salvador.* Washington, DC: Washington Office on Latin America and Hemisphere Initiatives.

———. 1996a. "International Tutelage and Domestic Political Will: Building a New Civilian Police Force in El Salvador." In *Policing Change, Changing Policing,* ed. O. Marenin. New York: Garland.

———. 1996b. *Protectors or Perpetrators? The Institutional Crisis of the Salvadoran Civilian Police.* Washington, DC: Washington Office on Latin America/Hemisphere Initiatives.

Stanley, W., and R. Lossle. 1998. "Peace and Public Insecurity: The Civilian Police Component of the Peace Operations in El Salvador." In *Policing the New World Disorder,* ed. R. B. Oakley, M. J. Dziedzic, and E. M. Goldberg, 67–108. Washington, DC: National Defense University.

Stephens, M. 1994. "Care and Control: The Future of British Policing." *Policing and Society* 4 (3): 237–251.

Stromsem, J. 1997. "Request for Information on ICITAP's Mission and Vision." Memorandum, Deputy Attorney General, Washington, DC, November 14.

Stromsem, J. 2000. "Comprehensive Strategic Planning Framework: A Practical Guide to Strategic Planning for Judicial Reform." Unpublished paper.

Stromsem, J. M., and Joseph Trincellito. 2003. "Building the Haitian National Police: A Retrospective and Prospective View." Washington, DC: Trinity College, Program in International Affairs.

Swedish National Police Board. 2000. *IPTF: The International Police Task Force, 1998–1999—A Report on the State of Things.* Stockholm, Sweden: Swedish National Police Board.

Taub, J. 2004. "Making Sense of the Mission." *New York Times Magazine.* April 11.

Thomas, L., and S. Spataro. 1998. "Peacekeeping and Policing in Somalia." In *Policing the New World Disorder*, ed. R. Oakley, M. Dziedzic, and E. M. Goldberg. Washington, DC: National Defense University.

Thompson, Robert. 1969. *No Exit from Vietnam.* London: Chatto and Windus.

Toch, Hans. 1980. "Mobilizing Police Expertise." *The Annals* 452 (November): 53–62.

———. 2002. *Stress in Policing.* Washington, DC: American Psychological Association.

Tonry, M., and N. Morris, eds. *Modern Policing.* Chicago: University of Chicago Press.

Trojanowicz, R., and B. Bucqueroux. 1990. *Community Policing: A Contemporary Perspective.* Cincinnati, OH: Anderson.

Tyler, T. 1990. *Why People Obey the Law.* New Haven, CT: Yale University Press.

Tyler, Tom R. 1997. "Procedural Fairness and Compliance with the Law." *Swiss Journal of Economics and Statistics* 133: 219–240.

United Nations. 2000. *Principles and Guidelines for United Nations Civilian Police.* Draft report, United Nations, New York.

———. 2001. *UNDP Security Sector Reform Assistance in Post-Conflict Situations: Lessons Learned in El Salvador, Guatemala, Haiti, Mozambique, Somalia, and Rwanda.* New York: United Nations, Emergency Response Division.

———. 2002a (June). *Report of the Secretary-General on the United Nations Mission in Bosnia and Herzegovina.* New York: United Nations.

———. 2002b (October). *Monthly Summary of Military and Civilian Police Contribution to United Nations Operations.* http://www.un.org.

United Nations, Department of Peacekeeping Operations. 1999. *Report on the Follow-up Workshop on Civilian Police in United Nations Peacekeeping.* New York: United Nations.

United Nations Commissioner for Human Rights. 1996. *International Human Rights Standards for Law Enforcement: A Pocket Book on Human Rights for the Police.* Geneva, Switzerland.

United Nations Development Programme. 2001. *UNDP Security Sector Reform Assistance in Post-Conflict Situations: Lessons Learned in El Salvador, Guatemala, Haiti, Mozambique, Somalia, and Rwanda.* New York: United Nations, Emergency Response Division.

———. 2002. *Human Development Report.* New York: United Nations.

United Nations Mission in Bosnia and Herzegovina. 1996a. *Commissioner's Guidance for Democratic Policing in the Federation of Bosnia-Herzegovina.* Sarajevo, BiH: UNMIK.

———. 1996b. *Principles of Democratic Policing.* Sarajevo, BiH: UNMIK.

———. 2002. *Mandate Implementation Plan: Action Plan.* Sarajevo, BiH: United Nations.

U.S. Agency for International Development. 1994. "USAID Policy on Police Assistance: Memo to the Administrator." Memorandum, Rule of Law Working Group, Washington, DC.

———. 1998a. *Civil-Military Relations: USAID's Role.* Washington, DC: Center for Democracy and Governance.

———. 1998b. *Handbook of Democracy and Governance Program Indicators.* Washington, DC: USAID, Center for Democracy and Governance.

———. 2002. "Position Paper on Policing Assistance." Washington, DC. Confidential.

U.S. Agency for International Development Rule of Law Working Group. 1994. "USAID Policy on Police Assistance." Internal memo, November 14.

U.S. Department of Defense and U.S. Department of State. 2003. *Foreign Military Training and DOD Engagement Activities of Interest: Joint Report to Congress.* Washington, DC: DOD.

U.S. Department of Justice. 2001. *Principles for Promoting Police Integrity: Examples of Promising Police Practices and Policies.* Washington, DC: U.S. Department of Justice.

U.S. Department of Justice, Criminal Division. 2002. *ICITAP, BiH Program.* Internal report, June 14.

U.S. Department of State. 2000. *White Paper: The Clinton Administration's Policy on Strengthening Criminal Justice Agencies in Support of Peace Operations.* Washington, DC: U.S. Department of State.

———. 2003. *Fact Sheet: US Participation in International Police (CIVPOL) Missions.* Washington, DC: U.S. Department of State.

U.S. Department of State, Bureau of International Narcotics and Law Enforcement Affairs. 2002–2006. *Fiscal Year Budgets: Congressional Justification.* Washington, DC: U.S. Department of State.

U.S. Department of State, Office of the Coordinator of U.S. Assistance to Europe and Eurasia. 2003. *U.S. Government Assistance and Cooperative Activities with Eurasia, FY 2002.* Washington, DC: U.S. Department of State.

U.S. General Accounting Office. 1992. *Foreign Aid: Police Training and Assistance.* Washington, DC: GAO/NSAID-92–118.

———. 1993. *Foreign Assistance: Meeting the Training Needs of Police in New Democracies.* A report to Congressional Requesters. Washington, DC: GAO.

———. 1999. *Foreign Assistance: Rule of Law Funding Worldwide for Fiscal Years 1993–1998.* Washington, DC: GAO, National Security and International Affairs Division.

———. 2001. *Former Soviet Union: U.S. Rule of Law Assistance Has Had Limited Impact.* Washington, DC: GAO.

———. 2002. *Foreign Assistance: Any Further Aid to Haitian Justice System Should Be Linked to Performance-Related Conditions.* Washington, DC: GAO.

———. 2003. *Foreign Assistance: U.S. Democracy Programs in Six Latin American Countries Have Yielded Modest Results.* Washington, DC: GAO.

U.S. Institute of Peace. 2001. *American Civilian Police in UN Peace Operations: Lessons Learned and Ideas for the Future.* Washington, DC: U.S. Institute of Peace.

———. 2004. *Building Civilian Capacity for U.S. Stability Operations: The Rule of Law Component.* Special report 118. Washington, DC: USIP.

Van Creveld, M. 1991. *The Transformation of War*. New York: The Free Press.

Van der Spuy, E. 1997. *Transnationalism in Policing: A Report on Recent Developments*. Capetown, South Africa: University of Capetown, Institute of Criminology.

———. 1999. "International Assistance to Police Reform: Observations from South Africa." Unpublished paper, University of Capetown, Department of Criminology, Capetown, South Africa.

VERA Institute of Justice. 2003. *Measuring Progress toward Safety and Justice: A Global Guide to the Design of Performance Indicators across the Justice Sector*. New York: VERA Institute of Justice.

Walker, Samuel. 1989. *Sense and Nonsense about Crime*, 2nd ed. Pacific Grove, CA: Brooks/Cole.

———. 2001. *Police Accountability*. Belmont, CA: Wadsworth Publishing.

Warner, M. 2000. "SFOR Lessons Learned in Creating a Secure Environment with Respect for the Rule of Law: Based on a Study of Bosnia." Washington, DC: Unpublished paper.

Washington Office on Latin America. 1995. *Demilitarizing Public Order: The International Community, Police Reform and Human Rights in Central America and Haiti*. Washington, DC: WOLA.

Washington Office on Latin America and the American University School of International Service. 1990. *Elusive Justice: The U.S. Administration of Justice Program in Latin America*. Washington, DC: WOLA.

Wedel, J. R. 1998. *Collision and Collusion: The Strange Case of Western Aid to Eastern Europe 1989–1998*. New York: St. Martin's.

Wentz, L., ed. 1997. *Lessons from Bosnia: The IFOR Experience*. Washington, DC: Department of Defense, Command and Control Research Program.

White, T. W., and R. A. Gillice. 1977. *Neighborhood Team Policing in Boulder, Colorado—A Case Study*. Washington, DC: The Urban Institute.

Wilson, D. G., and W. F. Walsh. 1997. "Reflections on the Transfer of Knowledge to Support Democratic Policing in Hungary and Romania." In *Policing in Emerging Democracies: Workshop Papers and Highlights*. Washington, DC: National Institute of Justice, Department of State.

Woodward, S. L. 1995. *Balkan Tragedy*. Washington, DC: The Brookings Institution.

World Bank. 1999. *Consultations with the Poor*. Washington, DC: The World Bank.

World Bank Group. 2002. "Worldwide Governance Research Indicators Dataset." http://www.worldbank.org/wbi/governance/govdata2002/index.html.

Wulf, D. H. 2000. *Security-Sector Reform in Developing Countries: An Analysis of the International Debate and Potentials for Implementing Reforms with Recommendations for Technical Cooperation*. Bonn, Germany: Deutsche Gesellschaft für Technische Zusammenarbeit (GTZ).

Zakharia, Fareed. 2001. "There's More to Right than Might." *Newsweek*, July 9.

Zeller, T. 2003. "Building Democracy Is Not a Science." *New York Times*, April 27, sec. A3.

Zoufal, D. R. 1999. *Restructuring the Police in Bosnia-Herzegovina*. Draft.

Index